BLITZ CATALOGING WORKBOOK

CATALOGING NONPRINT MATERIALS

Other Blitz Cataloging Workbooks

MARC/AACR2/Authority Control Tagging
Subject Analysis

BLITZ CATALOGING WORKBOOK

CATALOGING NONPRINT MATERIALS

Bobby Ferguson
East Baton Rouge Parish Library

1999

Libraries Unlimited, Inc.

Englewood, Colorado

LIBRARIES UNLIMITED, INC.
P.O. Box 6633
Englewood, CO 80155-6633
(800) 237-6124
www.lu.com

Ron Maas, *Acquisitions Editor*
Constance Hardesty, *Project Manager*
Brooke Graves, *Editor*
Sheryl Tongue, *Design and Composition*

Library of Congresss Cataloging-in-Publication Data

Ferguson, Anna S.
    Cataloging nonprint materials : blitz cataloging workbook / Bobby Ferguson.
    xii, 169 p. 22×28 cm.
    ISBN 1-56308-642-5
    1. Cataloging of nonbook materials--United States--Problems, exercises, etc.
  2. Descriptive cataloging--United States--Rules--Problems, exercises, etc.
  3. Anglo-American cataloguing rules--Problems, exercises, etc. I. Title.
  Z695.66.F47   1998
  025.3'4--dc21   98-19548
                                                              CIP

Table of Contents

Acknowledgments

I would like to express my appreciation and gratitude to Tom Jaques, Mickey McKann, and Elisabeth Spanhoff of the State Library of Louisiana; Anna Marchiafava of the West Baton Rouge Parish Library; Anna Wade and Raffy Rigney for the map cataloging; Lihong Zhu for the videorecording cataloging; Gary Ferguson for help with the wording and proofing, and for his continuing friendship; and the best editor in the world, Sheila Intner, for all her help, friendship, and knowledge. Thank you all.

BLITZ CATALOGING WORKBOOK SERIES
Introduction

Cataloging and classification are the most important parts of librarianship. Without a catalog, either manual or electronic, a library is no more than a room full of books and cannot provide services to its patrons in a reliable, timely fashion. Other library activities such as acquisition of new materials, interlibrary lending, and reference cannot be accomplished if patrons and staff cannot find out what a particular library contains.

Knowledge of cataloging is important to all librarians, not just catalogers. As more and more libraries become automated, a knowledge of MARC fields and electronic formats, as well as call numbers and subject headings, is essential and will make all librarians more proficient. Using these workbooks should cause you to absorb a lot of information that will be useful to you in any library situation.

As for catalogers, you will find that you cannot do a superior job as a beginning cataloger. Experience is necessary, preferably under an experienced cataloger. These workbooks are intended to reinforce your knowledge of the fundamentals of cataloging. They will help you to understand the MARC format and functions of the various fields and subfields; to evaluate copy cataloging and classification of various formats of materials; to locate errors and inconsistencies; to learn access points and which are the most important; to assign subject headings using both *Library of Congress Subject Headings* and *Sears List of Subject Headings*; to assign call numbers in both Dewey and LC classification schedules; and to evaluate and construct cross-references and authority headings.

Cataloging Nonprint Materials
INTRODUCTION

Being asked to catalog nonprint materials frightens a lot of beginning catalogers; indeed, it frightens a lot of experienced catalogers, also. In reality, it is no different from cataloging books—a few fields are different, such as scale for maps or technical specifications for computer files, but the rest of the bibliographic record is basically the same as for books. The physical description field, for example, still has only four subfields: extent of item, other details, size, and accompanying materials. The imprint field still has only three subfields: place of publication, publisher, and date. Subject headings remain basically the same, and other areas (such as series, added entries, and so on) are found in nonprint cataloging as well as in monographic cataloging.

There are differences, of course. Notes fields can contain many different types of information depending on the type of material. Although notes fields exist to give additional information about the item being cataloged, the content of the notes can be quite different. Nonprint materials also contain general material designations, or GMDs, which tell the general type of material being cataloged. These GMDs are found in rule 1.1C1 in the *Anglo-American Cataloguing Rules*, 2nd edition, 1988 revision (*AACR2R*). Being "general," they are not specific. The specific material designation, or SMD, goes in the physical description field. For example, for audio materials the GMD is **sound recording**. The SMDs are **sound disc, sound cassette, sound cartridge, sound tape reel,** and **sound track film.**

This workbook covers videorecordings, sound recordings, computer files, maps, and kits. There is an additional chapter with exercises for other types of materials, such as art prints, realia, microforms, and flash cards, but the majority of the workbook covers the basic five types. It includes sample records, tagging exercises, error identification, and specific *AACR2R* rules for each type of material. 008 field (header) information is also given, with examples for each type of material.

Some cataloging modules place the coded data given in the header, or 008 field, in a single line at the head of the MARC record. In contrast, some of the bibliographic utilities, such as OCLC, put this information in a generic form at the top of the MARC record. An example of an OCLC record is given on page xii. After that are examples of bibliographic records for different nonprint formats that display the header information in an 008 field.

OCLC: 30502954   Rec stat: c

Entered: 19940527   Replaced: 19940527   Used: 19940527

Type: e   Bib lvl: m   Source: d   Lang: eng

RecG: a   Enc lvl: I   Govt pub: Ctry: sdu

Relief: Mod rec: Base: ^^^   Form:

Desc: Indx: 0   Dat tp: s   Dates: 1993,

1	040	*** ≠c ***
2	007	a ≠b r ≠d a ≠e a ≠f z ≠g b ≠h a
3	034 1	a ≠b 1000000 ≠d W0820000 ≠e W0800000 ≠f N0263000 ≠g N0253000
4	052	3932 ≠b E89
5	052	3934 ≠b M5 ≠b N2
6	090	G3932.E89A4 1973 ≠b .E7
7	110 2	EROS Data Center.
8	245 10	[LANDSAT satellite image]. ≠n E-1242-15240-5, ≠p [Everglades region, Florida].
9	255	Scale 1:1,000,000. ≠c (W 82°00'--W 80°00'/N 26°30'--N 25°30').
10	260	[Sioux Falls, S.D.] : ≠b NASA, ≠c 1973.
11	300	1 remote-sensing image ; ≠c 22 × 22 cm.
12	500	Shows southern portion of the Florida peninsula, Lake Okeechobee to Everglades to Florida Bay (N-S) and Miami to Naples (E-W).
13	500	"Path 16, row 42"--index.
14	500	"22MAR73"
15	500	Title devised by cataloger.
16	500	Oriented with north to the upper left.
17	500	"C N25-59/W080-55 N N25-59/W080-48 MSS 5 D SUN EL50 AZ124 189-3373-N-1-N-D-2L NASA ERTS"
18	500	Glossy monochrome photograph on Kodak paper.
19	651 0	Everglades Region (Fla.) ≠x Photo maps.
20	651 0	Miami Region (Fla.) ≠x Photo maps.
21	651 0	Naples Region (Fla.) ≠x Photo maps.
22	650 0	Remote sensing ≠z Florida ≠z Everglades Region ≠x Maps.
23	650 0	Remote sensing ≠z Florida ≠z Miami Region ≠x Maps.
24	650 0	Remote sensing ≠z Florida ≠z Naples Region ≠x Maps.
25	710 1	United States. ≠b National Aeronautics and Space Administration.

1.
GENERAL INFORMATION

This chapter provides examples of cataloging for various nonprint materials, indicators, tagging exercises, general error identification exercises, and information about the 008 field.

1.1. Examples of Records for Various Nonprint Materials

Videorecording

008	921201s1990 . . . . nyu031 . c . . . . vceng . d
245 04	≠a The Titanic, lost... and found ≠h [videorecording].
260	≠a New York : ≠b Random House Video, ≠c 1990.
300	≠a 1 videocassette (31 min.) : ≠b sd., col. ; ≠c 1/2 in.
440 0	≠a Famous shipwrecks video series
500	≠a Title from title screen.
511	≠a Narrated by Brad Pitt.
500	≠a Based on the book by Judy Donnelly.
650 0	≠a Titanic (Steamship)
700 1	≠a Pitt, Brad.
700 1	≠a Donnelly, Judy.

Sound Recording

008	950108s1994 . . . . nyunnn . c . . . . g . . . eng . d
100 1	≠a Donnelly, Judy.
245 14	≠a The Titanic, lost... and found ≠h [sound recording] / ≠c Judy Donnelly.
260	≠a New York : ≠b Random House Audio, ≠c p1987.
300	≠a 1 sound cassette (21 min.) : ≠b mono.
440 0	≠a Famous shipwrecks audio series
511	≠a Narrated by John Denver.
650 0	≠a Titanic (Steamship)
700 1	≠a Denver, John.

008	971012s1992 . . . . tnucrn . e . . . . eng . d
245 00	≠a Christmas in the king's court ≠h [sound recording] : ≠b Celtic harp and pan flute / ≠c harpist Ann Heymann ; pan flute Robert Windenhill.
260	≠a Nashville, TN : ≠b Silver Bells, ≠c p1992.
300	≠a 1 sound disk (ca. 35 min.) : ≠b digital, stereo. ; ≠c 4 3/4 in.
505 0	≠a Angels we have heard on high -- What child is this -- Joy to the world -- Love came down at Christmas/Long ago & far away -- First noel -- Deck the halls -- Hark the herald angels sing -- Away in a manger -- It came upon a midnight clear -- Silent night/O holy night -- O come all ye faithful -- O little town of Bethlehem.
650 0	≠a Christmas music.
650 0	≠a Flute music.
650 0	≠a Harp music.
700 1	≠a Heymann, Ann.
700 1	≠a Windenhill, Robert.

Computer File

245 04	≠a The orchestra ≠h [interactive multimedia] : ≠b the instruments revealed.
246 3	≠a Young person's guide to the orchestra.
256	≠a Computer data and program
260	≠a Burbank, CA : ≠b Warner New Media, ≠c c1991.
300	≠a 1 computer optical disc : ≠b sd. ; ≠c 4 3/4 in. + ≠e instruction booklet.
440 0	≠a Warner audio notes
538	≠a System requirements: Macintosh computer; at least 2M of memory; system software 6.0.5 or later; HyperCard 2.0 or greater; hard disk drive with at least 4.5M of free space; audio playback equipment; Apple CD SC CD-ROM drive (or compatible).
500	≠a Title from disc label.
500	≠a Music plays as pure audio on regular CD players.
520	≠a An interactive multimedia introduction to instruments of the orchestra featuring the 1964 recording of Benjamin Britten's The young person's guide to the orchestra, Op. 34, with the composer conducting the London Symphony Orchestra. Through the music, photographs, on-screen commentary and annotation, historical information, sounds, and musical analysis, users see what instruments look like, hear how they sound, and learn how they are played.
600 10	≠a Britten, Benjamin, ≠d 1913-1976. ≠t Young person's guide to the orchestra ≠x Analysis, appreciation ≠x Interactive multimedia.
650 0	≠a Orchestra ≠x Interactive multimedia.
650 0	≠a Musical instruments ≠x Interactive multimedia.
700 10	≠a Britten, Benjamin, ≠d 1913-1976. ≠t Young person's guide to the orchestra. ≠f 1991.

Map

008		950523s1817 . . . . xx . . . . a . . f . . 0 . . . eng . d
110	1	≠a United States. ≠b Topographical Bureau.
245	10	≠a Plan and profiles of the remains of the fort at Baton Rouge ≠h [map] / ≠c United States Engineering Dept., Topographical Bureau.
255		≠a Scale 1:[300]
260		≠a [S.l. : ≠b s.n.], ≠c 1817.
300		≠a 1 map : ≠b photocopy ; ≠c 37 × 58 cm.
500		≠a Oriented with North to the left.
500		≠a Scale is given as 100 yards to 1 foot for both the scale of the plan and the scale of the profile.
651	0	≠a Fort Baton Rouge (La.) ≠x Maps.
651	0	≠a Baton Rouge (La.) ≠x Maps.

Kit

008		960430s1995 . . . . lau . . . . eng . d
100	1	≠a Ferguson, Terre.
245	12	≠a A packet for the Bank of West Baton Rouge ≠h [kit] / ≠c designed and created by Terre Ferguson.
260		≠a Port Allen, La. : ≠b Bank of West Baton Rouge, ≠c c1995.
300		≠a 1 chart, 1 sound cassette, 1 diorama, 1 script (5 copies), 22 slides (in carousel), 1 guide (2 copies) ; in container 28 × 32 × 18 cm.
500		≠a Created to be an orientation tool for new employees at the Bank of West Baton Rouge, Port Allen, Louisiana.
610	20	≠a Bank of West Baton Rouge.

Art Reproduction

100	1	≠a Smith, Joey.
245	10	≠a Animals of the jungle ≠h [art reproduction] / ≠c drawn by Joey Smith.
260		≠a New York : ≠b Art Prints Inc., ≠c 1996.
300		≠a 1 art print : ≠b col. ; ≠c 25 × 38 in.
440	0	≠a Animals of the world
500		≠a Matted with 2-inch white border all around.
650	0	≠a Animals ≠z Africa.

Art Original

100	1	≠a Ferguson, Alan.
245	10	≠a Portrait of a young girl ≠h [art original] / ≠c drawn by Alan Ferguson.
260		≠c 1996.
300		≠a 1 painting : ≠b oil, col. ; ≠c 16 × 20 in.
500		≠a Portrait of the artist's daughter, Erin Elizabeth Ferguson, at the age of seven.
600	10	≠a Ferguson, Erin Elizabeth.
650	0	≠a Art, American.

Filmstrip

245 00	≠a Groundhog's day ≠h [filmstrip].	
260	≠a Chicago, IL : ≠b Society for Visual Education, ≠c 1980.	
300	≠a 1 filmstrip (38 fr.) : ≠b col. ; ≠c 35 mm. + ≠e 1 sound cassette.	
500	≠a Sound accompaniment compatible with manual operation only.	
650 0	≠a Groundhogs ≠x Fiction.	
650 0	≠a Holidays.	

1.2. Indicators

100 _ Personal name	110 _ Corporate name	111 _ Conference
0 Single forename	1 Place name	2 Direct
1 Surname	2 Direct order	
3 Family name *[630 only]*		

245 _ _	1st indicator: Title tracing 1=Yes, 0=No 2nd indicator: Number of spaces to skip in indexing
250	Indicators are blank
260	Indicators are blank
300	Indicators are blank
400, 410, 411	Same first indicator as 1xx
440 _	Series title traced, 2nd indicator, no. of spaces skipped
490 _	Series title not traced, or traced differently 1st indicator: 0=not traced, 1=traced differently
500	Indicators are blank
504	Indicators are blank
505 _	1st indicator: 0=entire contents, 1=partial contents, 2=incomplete contents
520	Indicators are blank
6xx _	Second indicator 0=*LCSH*, 1=Annotated cards, 8=*Sears*
600, 610, 611	Same 1st indicators as 1xx field
650, 651	No 1st indicator
7xx	1st indicator same as 1xx
740 _ _	1st indicator 0; 2nd indicator is 2 [analytical entry]
8xx	Series traced differently.

Audiovisual items are almost always title main entry. Sound recordings vary.

1.3. General Nonprint Tagging Exercises

Add the proper tags, indicators, and subfields to the data given in each question. The blanks indicate where tags, indicators, and subfields should be placed. Precede each subfield code with a delimiter. You will need to use the USMARC bibliographic formats, *AACR2R*, *Library of Congress Subject Headings (LCSH)*, or other tools. The first one in each section has been done for you.

Main Entries

1.3.1.   100 1   ǂa Jones, Jessie.

1.3.2.   1_ _   ____ Fitzgerald-Hughes, Edmund.

1.3.3.   1_ _   ____ Utah. ____ Legislature. ____ House of Representatives.

1.3.4.   1_ _   ____ Alabama Museum of Natural History.

1.3.5.   1_ _   ____ Athabasca National Forest.

1.3.6.   1_ _   ____ Petrovsky, Alexandrovitch, ____ 1902-

1.3.7.   1_ _   ____ Spears, John J. ____ (John Julius), ____ 1899-1942.

1.3.8.   1_ _   ____ Timothy, ____ of Jerusalem.

1.3.9.   1_ _   ____ Bee Gees (Musical group)

1.3.10.   1_ _   ____ Kansas City (Kans.). ____ Police Jury.

1.3.11.   1_ _   ____ Regional Planning Council for Southwest Louisiana.

1.3.12.   1_ _   ____ Ford, Gerald R.

1.3.13.   1_ _   ____ Pennywhistle, John, ____ Sir, ____ 1802-1901.

1.3.14.   1_ _   ____ Monroe Bowling Tournament ____ (1983 : Monroe, La.)

Title Statements

1.3.15.   245 0 _   ǂa Faust ǂh [videorecording].

1.3.16.   245 _ _   ____ The body in the wall ____ [sound recording] / ____ Joe Boyd.

1.3.17.   245 _ _   ____ Sunny days ____ [picture] / ____ Elizabeth Crane.

1.3.18.   245 _ _   ____ The vampire companion ____ [slide] / ____ Anne Rice.

1.3.19.   245 _ _   ____ The "screech and howl" Halloween record ____ [sound recording] / ____ by the Screamers.

1.3.20.   245 _ _   ____ Niewe Amsterdamsegids ____ [sound recording] = ____ Guide to New Amsterdam / ____ by E. de Rijk Spanhoff.

1.3.21.   245 _ _   ____ BASIC programming ____ [computer file] / ____ Nancy Davis.

1.3.22.   245 _ _   ____ Underneath the oceans of the world ____ [globe].

1.3.23.   245 _ _   ____ Forest scenes ____ [realia] / ____ by Al Gore.

1.3.24.   245 _ _   ____ Fort Claiborne ____ [map] / ____ drawn by Cecil Atkinson.

1.3.25.   245 _ _   ____ The body in detail ____ [model] / ____ Will Tryon ... [et al.].

1.3.26.   245 _ _   ____ Family papers ____ [microform] / ____ Sir Matthew Hale.

1.3.27.   245 _ _   ____ Subtraction ____ [flash card] / ____ Chris Sharp.

Publication, Distribution, etc.

1.3.28.	260	_≠a_	Englewood, Colo. : _≠b_ Libraries Unlimited, _≠c_ [1949].
1.3.29.	260	____	Washington D.C. : ____ U.S. Department of Education : [for sale by the U.S. G.P.O.], ____ 1975.
1.3.30.	260	____	London : ____ Haynes ; ____ Brookstone, Conn. : ____ Auto Museum, ____c1997.
1.3.31.	260	____	[Monterey, Mass.?] : ____ Matthew Intner, ____ 1986.
1.3.32.	260	____	[Baton Rouge] : ____ Louisiana State University Press, ____ 1985.

Physical Description

1.3.33.	300	_≠a_	1 videodisc (35 min.) : _≠b_ sd., col., 1500 rpm ; _≠c_ 8 in.
1.3.34.	300	____	64 flash cards ; ____ 22 × 10 cm.
1.3.35.	300	____	1 videorecording (65 min.) : ____ sd., b&w ; ____ 1/2 in.
1.3.36.	300	____	10 sound cassettes (15 hrs.) : ____ mono.
1.3.37.	300	____	1 diorama (various pieces) : ____ plywood and papier mache ; 18 × 28 × 12 cm.
1.3.38.	300	____	1 videocassette (22 min.) : ____ sd., col. ; ____ 1/2 in.
1.3.39.	300	____	1 microscope slide : ____ glass ; ____ 8 × 3 cm.
1.3.40.	300	____	1 game (15 pieces) : ____ col., cardboard ; ____ 9 × 12 in.
1.3.41.	300	____	1 sound disc (47 min.) : ____ stereo. ; ____ 12 in.
1.3.42.	300	____	2 film reels (60 min. ea.) : ____ sd., b&w ; ____ 16 mm.
1.3.43.	300	____	2 books, 1 carousel of slides, 3 transparencies, 2 workbooks (15 copies each), 1 guide (4 copies)
1.3.44.	300	____	1 score : ____ 16 p. of music ; ____ 28 cm.
1.3.45.	300	____	15 maps : ____ col. ; ____ 26-54 cm.
1.3.46.	300	____	1 sound disc (65 min.) : ____ digital, stereo. ; ____ 4 3/4 in.
1.3.47.	300	____	1 art reproduction : ____ lithograph, col. ; ____ image 33 × 41 cm., on sheet 46 × 57 cm.
1.3.48.	300	____	1 art original : ____ pastel on paper ; ____ 22 × 28 cm.

Series Statement

1.3.49.	4_40_ _0	_≠a_	Preservation guide
1.3.50.	4_ __	____	Fodor video guides
1.3.51.	4_ __	____	Nicholls State University. ____ Center for Traditional Louisiana Boatbuilding. ____ Wooden boat series
1.3.52.	4_ __	____	Electronic report / University of Southwestern Louisiana, Center for Archaeological Studies
1.3.53.	4_ __	____	Water resources series. ____ North Louisiana subseries

Notes

1.3.54.   *500*   *≠a*   Title from disk label.

1.3.55.   *5__*   ____   Summary: Shaquille O'Neal's greatest moves as a professional basketball player.

1.3.56.   *5__*   ____   With: Only in your arms / Lisa Kleypas.

1.3.57.   *5__*   ____   Includes discography (p. 547-569).

1.3.58.   *5__*   ____   Title supplied by cataloger.

1.3.59.   *5__*   ____   Videorecording of the motion picture from 1944.

1.3.60.   *5__*   ____   Cast: Ronald Reagan, Bill Clinton, Richard Nixon.

1.3.61.   *5__*   ____   Contents: Hey look me over -- Louisiana hayride -- Cajun two-step -- When the saints go marching in -- Bayou blues -- LSU alma mater.

1.3.62.   *5__*   ____   Producers, Bill Gates and Bill Clinton ; music, Bill Conti ; screenplay, Bill Graham ; director, Bill Smith.

1.3.63.   *5__*   ____   Includes 1 computer disk.

1.3.64.   *5__*   ____   Includes subtitles in English.

Subject Descriptors

1.3.65.   *600 1 0*   *≠a*   Nixon, Richard M.

1.3.66.   *6__ __*   ____   Gardening ____ Louisiana ____ New Orleans.

1.3.67.   *6__ __*   ____   Louisiana. ____ Office of the Lieutenant Governor.

1.3.68.   *6__ __*   ____   State Library of Louisiana. ____ Technical Services Branch.

1.3.69.   *6__ __*   ____   Cookery (Oysters)

1.3.70.   *6__ __*   ____   Daughters of the Confederacy. ____ Louisiana Chapter. ____ Baton Rouge Post.

1.3.71.   *6__ __*   ____   Port Allen (La.) ____ Politics and government.

1.3.72.   *6__ __*   ____   Alexandria (La.) ____ History ____ Civil War, 1861-1865.

1.3.73.   *6__ __*   ____   Lawrence, Elizabeth, ____ 1904-1985.

1.3.74.   *6__ __*   ____   Physically handicapped artists ____ Louisiana.

1.3.75.   *6__ __*   ____   Ferguson family.

1.3.76.   *6__ __*   ____   Paul M. Hebert Law Center.

1.3.77.   *6__ __*   ____   Lafourche Parish (La.) ____ Description and travel.

1.3.78.   *6__ __*   ____   Lafayette Parish (La.). ____ Office of the Mayor.

1.3.79.   *6__ __*   ____   New Tickfaw Baptist Church (Livingston Parish, La.)

1.3.80.   *6__ __*   ____   Joan, ____ of Arc, Saint.

1.3.81.   *6__ __*   ____   Pilottown (La.) ____ History.

1.3.82.   *6__ __*   ____   Hunter, Bruce, ____ 1958-

1.3.83.   *6__ __*   ____   East Feliciana Parish (La.) ____ Economic aspects.

1.3.84.   *6__ __*   ____   Hurricanes ____ Louisiana ____ Cheniere Caminada.

1.3.85.   *6__ __*   ____   Grand Isle Tarpon Rodeo ____ (26th : ____ 1979)

1.3.86.   *6__ __*   ____   Bible. ____ O.T. ____ Genesis.

1.4. General Error Identification Exercises

There is one error on each line. The errors will be in the tag, the indicators, or the subfields. Circle the error, then write the correction above the error.

1.4.1.   110 1   ≠a Smith, John, ≠d 1956-

1.4.2.   130 1   ≠a Garcia Williams, John.

1.4.3.   110 2   ≠a Omaha (Neb.). ≠b Parish Council.

1.4.4.   100 2   ≠a Ann Margaret, ≠d 1943-

1.4.5.   111 1   ≠a Harpsichord championship ≠d (1995)

1.4.6.   245 10   ≠a Solemn moments ≠h [sound recording].

1.4.7.   240 10   ≠a The horse jumps ≠h [kit].

1.4.8.   245 10   ≠b Everybody wins! ≠h [map] / ≠c Polly Tishan.

1.4.9.   246 14   ≠a You @#$%^&*!!! ≠h [videorecording].

1.4.10.   245 12   ≠a A man for all seasons ≠h [computer file].

1.4.11.   260   ≠a New York : ≠b c1996.

1.4.12.   260   ≠a Libraries Unlimited, ≠c c1996.

1.4.13.   260   ≠a Omaha, Neb. : ≠b Windy Press, ≠d c1990.

1.4.14.   260 0   ≠a Gem, KS : ≠b J.W. Pub. Co., ≠c c1982.

1.4.15.   300   ≠a 1 map : ≠c col. ; ≠c 22 × 18 cm.

1.4.16.   300   ≠a 54 slides : ≠b sd. ; ≠c 35 cm.

1.4.17.   300   ≠a 1 doll : ≠b cloth ; ≠c 1965-

1.4.18.   301   ≠a 1 puzzle (13 pieces) : ≠b wood, col. ; ≠c 25 cm.

1.5. 008 (Header) Field, Nonprint Bibliographic Records

The header in bibliographic and authority records is used to record basic information such as the date the record was created, whether the work is juvenile, fiction, or biographical, and whether it is a government document. This information is given in field 008 and consists of forty character positions numbered 00–39, which contain defined data elements and provide coded information about the record as a whole or about special format aspects of the item being cataloged. Some indexing information is taken from the 008 field rather than the textual fields in the body of the record. Character positions 00–17 and 35–39 are the same for all formats; positions 18–34 are different for each format, with some exceptions. A data element common to more than one format always occupies the same character position in the record. For example, whenever a format has an element defined as **Government publication**, that element is in position 28. The Music format, for example, has no **Government publication** element, so position 28 is used for something else. The Maps format, in contrast, does have a **Government publication** element, which is in position 28. Positions 26–27 and 29–30 are currently undefined for the Maps format.

Undefined character positions contain either a blank (usually displayed in the bibliographic record as a dot (.) or a fill character (|). Each defined character position must contain either a defined code or one of the symbols discussed previously. The characters defined across all formats (positions 00–17 and 35–39), as well as positions 18–34 for each format, are given in the chapter for that format, immediately preceding the exercise on creating 008 fields. All codes (Country of publication code, Language code, and others) are taken from USMARC code lists.

2.

VIDEORECORDINGS

Videorecordings are found in the form of laser discs and videocassettes. Both are cataloged in the MARC Visual Materials format, as are films, filmstrips, and transparencies. *AACR2R*, however, divides these materials into two chapters: chapter 7 deals with motion pictures and videorecordings, and chapter 8 deals with graphic materials. Graphic materials include both opaque materials (art originals and reproductions, charts, photographs, technical drawings) and those intended to be projected or viewed (filmstrips, slides, transparencies), as well as collections of such graphic materials. As for all materials, *AACR2R* rules take precedence over the requirements of the MARC format.

Videorecordings are usually entered under title main entry, because responsibility for intellectual content cannot be attributed to one person. The director, the producer, the composer and musical director, the cast, the camera operators, the editor, and the writer all have responsibility for the final product, unlike a book, where the author is clearly responsible for the intellectual content.

A summary is usually included in the bibliographic record, because a videorecording cannot be browsed as a book can. Having the cast noted in the record is also useful, and subject headings can be of real importance in describing the work. Age level is usually given for educational videorecordings and should be added to the bibliographic record. If a Motion Picture Academy of America (MPAA) rating is present on the video or its container, it too should be given.

Other than the physical description, cataloging a videorecording is very much like cataloging a book. It's not really that difficult.

2.1. Videorecordings, Full Records Tagging Exercises

Add the proper tags, indicators, and subfields to the bibliographic records given here. The blanks indicate where tags, indicators, and subfields should be placed. Precede each subfield code with a delimiter. You will need to use the USMARC bibliographic formats, *AACR2R*, *LCSH*, and other tools.

2.1.1. 245 _ _   ____ Seasons of crawfish culture ____ [videorecording] / ____ Cooperative Extension Service ; written and produced by Lynn E. Dellenbarger.

260   ____ [Baton Rouge : ____ The Service?], ____ 1991.

300   ____ 1 videocassette (22 min.) : ____ sd., col. ; ____ 1/2 in.

500   ____ "January 1991".

538   ____ VHS format.

520   ____ Lynn Dellenbarger, a professor at LSU working with shellfish in Ag Economics, discusses crawfish culture and its economic aspects. Also discusses how the Cooperative Extension Service can help improve results.

610 _ _   ____ Louisiana Cooperative Extension Service.

650 _ _   ____ Crawfish ____ Louisiana.

650 _ _   ____ Agricultural extension work ____ Louisiana.

700 _ _   ____ Dellenbarger, Lynn E. ____ (Lynn Edwin), ____ 1953-

710 _   ____ Louisiana Cooperative Extension Service.

2.1.2. 245 _ _   ____ Fish 'n' bloopers ____ [videorecording] / ____ Strike King Productions.

246 _ _   ____ Fishing bloopers.

260   ____ [S.l.] : ____ Strike King Productions ; ____ St.-Laurent, Quebec : ____ Distributed by Madacy Music Group, ____ c1993.

300   ____ 1 videocassette (ca. 40 min.) : ____ sd., col. ; ____ 1/2 in.

500   ____ "Recorded in EP mode."

500   ____ Closed captioned for the hearing impaired.

500   ____ "BDO-3-4306"

511   ____ Starring Bill Dance.

520   ____ Contains outtakes from the television series "Bill Dance Outdoors" and "Unforgettable moments" with some of his special guests, including Hank Williams, Jr., Mel Tillis, Bobby Goldsboro, Terry Bradshaw, and others.

538   ____ VHS format.

650 _   ____ Fishing ____ Humor.

700 _   ____ Dance, Bill.

2.1.3. 2_ _ _ _   ____ Household consumption patterns for Louisiana crawfish ____ [videorecording] / ____ by Alvin Schopp and Lynn Dellenbarger.

2_ _   ____ [Baton Rouge] : ____ Louisiana Agricultural Experiment Station, ____ 1993.

3_ _   ____ 1 videocassette (21 min.) : ____ sd., col. ; ____ 1/2 in.

4_ _ _ _   ____ A.E.A. video information series

5_ _   ____ "May 1993".

5_ _   ____ VHS format.

5_ _   ____ Title from videocassette label.

5_ _   ____ A lecture about how much crawfish Louisianians eat, where they get it, and special ways of cooking it.

6_ _ _   ____ Crayfish.

6_ _ _   ____ Crayfish ____ Marketing.

6_ _ _   ____ Cookery (Crayfish)

7_ _ _   ____ Schopp, Alvin.

7_ _ _   ____ Dellenbarger, Lynn E. ____ (Lynn Edwin), ____ 1953-

7_ _ _   ____ Louisiana Agricultural Experiment Station.

2.1.4. 1_ _ _   ____ Short story in Louisiana.

2_ _ _ _   ____ The short story in Louisiana ____ [videocassette] / ____ edited by Mary Dell Fletcher.

2_ _   ____ 4th ed.

2_ _   ____ Lafayette, La. : ____ Center for Louisiana Studies, University of Southwestern Louisiana, ____ c1993.

3_ _   ____ 1 videocassette (20 min.) : ____ sd., col./b&w ; ____ 1/2 in.

5_ _   ____ VHS format.

5_ _   ____ A brief history of Louisiana short stories and the men and women who wrote them.

6_ _ _   ____ Short stories, American ____ Louisiana.

6_ _ _   ____ Louisiana ____ Fiction.

7_ _ _ _   ____ Fletcher, Mary Dell.

2.1.5. 1_ _ _   ____ Treasures of the Kingdom (Krewe).

2_ _ _ _   ____ 1994 Mardi Gras ball ____ [videorecording].

2_ _   ____ Lafayette, La. : ____ Treasures of the Kingdom, ____ c1994.

3_ _   ____ 1 videocassette (120 min.) : ____ sd., col. ; ____ 1/2 in.

5_ _   ____ Videographed by members of the Krewe.

5_ _   ____ VHS format.

5_ _   ____ Various members of the Lafayette Mardi Gras krewe videotaped their ball. Included are presentation of the court, entertainment by the Beach Boys, and costumes of the krewe members as the members of the krewe danced.

6_ _   _   ____ Carnival ____ Louisiana ____ Lafayette.

6_ _   _   ____ Costume ____ Louisiana ____ Lafayette.

2.1.6.   1_ _ _   ____ Ferguson, Bobby.

2_ _ _ _   ____ Travel and adventure in Outer Mongolia ____ [videorecording] / ____ Bobby Ferguson.

2_ _ _ _   ____ Outer Mongolia.

2_ _   ____ 1995.

3_ _   ____ 1 videocassette (45 min.) : ____ sd., col. ; ____ 1/2 in.

5_ _   ____ VHS format.

5_ _   ____ Bobby Ferguson videotaped her travels in Mongolia. Includes scenes from Ulaanbaatar, a nomad's ger (tent), Yoln Valley, the National Library of Mongolia, Gobi Desert, and much more.

6_ _   _   ____ Mongolia ____ Description and travel.

6_ _   _   ____ Gobi Desert.

6_ _   _   ____ Voyages and travels.

2.1.7.   _ _ _   ____ Trees in Baton Rouge ____ [videorecording].

_ _ _   ____ Baton Rouge trees, a guide to the city.

_   ____ 1st ed.

_   ____ Baton Rouge : ____ Louisiana Association of Nurserymen, ____ 1994.

_   ____ 1 videocassette (30 min.) : ____ sd., col. ; ____ 1/2 in.

_   ____ Project supported by an America the Beautiful grant from the Louisiana Dept. of Agriculture.

_   ____ Title on label: Baton Rouge trees, a guide to the city.

_   ____ VHS format.

_   ____ Includes specific subdivisions, specific trees, and tips for planting and growing exotic specimens.

_   _   ____ Trees in cities ____ Law and legislation ____ Louisiana.

_   _   ____ Louisiana Association of Nurserymen.

This one is all yours—no help, no tips, no blanks. Good luck.

2.1.8. _ _ _   Guillory, Vincent.

_ _ _   An evaluation of escape rings in blue crab traps [videorecording] / by Vincent Guillory, Jerry Merrell.

_   Bourg, La. : Marine Fisheries Division, Louisiana Dept. of Wildlife and Fisheries, 1993.

_   1 videocassette (15 min.) : sd., col. ; 1/2 in.

_ _   A.E.A. video technical bulletin

_   VHS format.

_   A taped lecture on trapping blue crabs.

_ _   Blue crabs.

_ _   Crab fisheries Louisiana.

_ _   Merrell, Jerry.

_ _   Louisiana. Marine Fisheries Division.

2.2. Videorecordings, Notes Exercise

Read section 7.7 in *Anglo-American Cataloguing Rules*, 2nd edition, 1988 revision. Use the order given there to put the notes in the bibliographic record below in the correct order. Number the notes from 1 to 9 on the blanks. The projected title is given in bold letters at the top of the set of notes.

Bayou passions

____   Summary: John sets out to wed Louisa, a daughter of the Lincolns who live at Wildwood Plantation, but runs into trouble when his former fiancee Ruby turns up.

____   With: Dirty pool.

____   VHS format.

____   Starring: John Wayne, Elizabeth Taylor, and Arnold Schwartzenegger.

____   Title on videocassette: Love on the bayou.

____   Distributed in the United States by: River Road Film & Video.

____   Also issued in 16mm film and Beta format.

____   Originally issued in the series: Sizzling sixties.

____   Documentary.

2.3. Videorecordings, Error Identification Exercises

The number of errors in each record is given in parentheses at the top of the record. Find the errors and circle them. Write the corrections above the errors. The errors may be in spelling, tags, indicators, subfields, punctuation, etc.

2.3.1. (14 errors)

245 04   ≠a Christmas in America [videorecording].

260 0   ≠a New York : ≠a Hyper Press, ≠c c1995.

300   ≠t 1 videorecording : ≠b sd., col. ; ≠c 16 mm.

400 0   ≠a Holiday series.

500   ≠a Narrated by David Wines.

500   ≠a VHS format.

651 0   ≠a Christmas ≠x United States.

700 20   ≠a Wines, David.

2.3.2. (8 errors)

245 00   ≠a The Scottish are coming! ≠h videorecording.

300 00   ≠a 2 videocassettes ≠t 120 min. : ≠b sd., col. ; ≠c 1/2 in.

500   ≠a Summary: Rehearsal of the programmed which the Scottish Black Watch

          Drum and Bugle Corps is planning to take on a world tour.

610 20   ≠ca Scottish Black Watch Drum and Bugle Corps.

2.3.3. (14 errors)

100 10   ≠a White, Ronald, ≠a 1944-

245 11   ≠a "How-to" on bodywork ≠h [videocassette] : car refinishing /

≠a SharpWhite Productions.

260 ≠a B.R., LA : ≠b SharpWhite Productions, ≠c 1987.

300 ≠a : ≠b, ≠c

511 ≠a Ronnie White and Sam Sharp demstrate how to get rid of bumps, lumps,

scratches, and dents in this absorbing demonstration of bodywork with an

Austin-Healy Sprite.

651 0 Automobiles ≠a Refinishing.

710 20 ≠a White, Ronald, ≠d 1944-

710 20 ≠a Sharp, Sam, ≠d 1943-

2.3.4. (11 errors)

245 10 ≠a Handling firearms ≠h [motion picture].

250 ≠a Schiller Park, Ill. : ≠b MTI Teleprograms, ≠c c1979.

300 ≠a 1 videorecording (32 min.) : ≠b sd., col. ; ≠c 1/2 in.

511 ≠C Production manager and special effects, Ron Adams ; director, Dennis

Anderson ; script, Charles Remsberg.

505 0 ≠a Covers the total range of tecknicques for safe handling of firearms. Shows

how to prevent accidental discharge, malfunction, and unintentional hits.

Discusses the consequences of wrong or faulty ammunition for law

enforcement personnel.

651 1 ≠a Firearms ≠a Safety measures.

650 0 ≠a Police officer training.

2.3.5. (14 errors)

245 04   Enemy alien ≠a [videorecording] / ≠c National Film Board of Canada.

246   ≠a 2nd ed.

260   ≠a [Quebec, Ont.] : ≠b The Board, ≠c c1795.

300   ≠a 3 videocassette (25 min.) : ≠b sd. ; ≠c 1/2 in.

508   ≠a Narrator: Stanley Jackson.

511   ≠a Producer, Wolf Koenig ; director, Jeanette Lerman ; music, Eldon Rathbone.

520   ≠a A documentary on Japanese internal during the Second World War.

650 4   ≠a Japanese Americans ≠y Evacuation and relocation.

700 10   ≠a National Film Board of Quebec.

2.3.6. (13 errors)

245 00   ≠t Computers and the quality of life / ≠c Regional Television Production

           Center, Moorhead State College.

260   ≠a Moosehead, Minn. : ≠b The Center, ≠cc p1973.

301   ≠a 1 videocassette (3333 min.) : ≠b sd., col. ; ≠c 1/2 in.

400 0   ≠t Communicating about computers to the educator ; ≠n no. 6

500   ≠a VSH format.

520   ≠a Discussion why the computer is a powerful social device, whether or not a

           computer can "think", and whether or not the computer enhances creativity.

600 5   ≠a Computers.

2.3.7. (13 errors)

245 00   ≠a In praise of hands ≠videorecording = Hommage aux mains.

246 10   ≠a Frommage aux mains.

260   ≠a Quebec, Canada : ≠b National Film Board of Canada, ≠c 1974.

300   ≠a 1 film reel (video) : ≠b sd., col. ; ≠c 1/2 in.

508   ≠a Vhs format.

538   ≠a Closed captioned for the visually impaired.

522   ≠a Shows people in various countries, including Japan, Nigeria, Mehico and

           Pland as they use their hands in creating works of craftsmanship.

650 0   ≠a Handicraft.

655 7   ≠a Decorative arts.

2.3.8. (1 error)

245 04   ≠a The sting ≠h [videorecording] / ≠c Universal Pictures.

260   ≠a Universal City, CAL : ≠b Universal Pictures, ≠c 1978.

300   ≠a 2 videocassettes (129 min.) : ≠b sd., col. ; ≠c 1/2 in.

511   ≠a Paul Newman, Robert Redford, Robert Shaw.

508   ≠a Producers: Tony Bill, Michael Phillips, Julia Phillips ; director, George Roy

           Hill ; writer David S. Ward.

500   ≠a Also issued as a motion picture.

520   ≠a Fast-paced comedy adventure story of two daring con men in Chicago in

the 1930s.

650 0   ≠a Feature films.

700 1   ≠a Newman, Paul.

700 1   ≠a Redford, Robert.

700 1   ≠a Shaw, Robert.

2.4. Videorecordings, 008 (Header) Information

The codes given here are specifically for videorecordings. Use them to create 008 fields for the records in the exercises following the code list.

00–05   Date entered on file; indicates the date the record was created; recorded in the pattern *yymmdd* (year/year/month/month/day/day).

06   Type of date/publication status. One-character code that categorizes the type of dates given in 008/07–10 (Date 1) and 008/11–14 (Date 2). For serials, 008/06 also indicates the publication status.

(blank)—No dates given; B.C. date involved. Each character in fields 008/07–10 and 008/11–14 contains a blank.

c—Serial item currently published. 008/07–10 contains the beginning date of publication; 008/11–14 contains 9999.

d—Serial item ceased publication. 008/07–10 contains beginning date of publication, 008/11–14 contains ending date.

e—Detailed date; 008/07–10 contains year and 008/11–14 contains month and day, recorded as *mmdd*.

i—Inclusive dates of collection.

k—Range of years of bulk of collection.

m—Multiple dates; 008/07–10 usually contains the beginning date and 008/11–14 contains the ending date.

n—Dates unknown; each position in 008/07–10 and 008/11–14 contains a blank.

p—Date of distribution/release/issue and production/recording session when different.

q—Questionable date; 008/07–10 contains the earliest possible date; 008/11–14 contains the latest possible date.

r—Reprint/reissue date and original date; 008/07–10 contains the date of reproduction or reissue (i.e., the most current date) and 008/11–14 contains the date of the original, if known.

s—Single known/probable date. 008/07–10 contains the date; 008/11–14 contains blanks.

t—Publication date and copyright date.

u—Serial status unknown. 008/07–10 contains the beginning date of publication; 008/11–14 contains 9999.

07–10 (Date 1)

(blank)—Date element is not applicable.

u—Date element is totally or partially unknown.

11–14 (Date 2)

(blank)—Date element is not applicable.

u—Date element is totally or partially unknown.

15–17 Place of publication, production, or execution. A two- or three-character code that indicates the place of publication, production, or execution. Two-character codes are left-justified and the unused position contains a blank. [Codes for the United States consist of the two-letter ZIP code abbreviation plus *u* for United States. New York, for example, would be coded *nyu*.] Unless otherwise specified, codes are always lower-case letters.

18–20 Running time for motion pictures and videorecordings. A three-digit number that indicates the total running time in minutes of the motion picture or videorecording. The number is right-justified and each unused position contains a zero.

000—Running time exceeds three characters

001–999—Running time

--- —Running time unknown

nnn—not applicable

21 Undefined. Contains a blank (.) or fill character (|).

22 Target audience.

(blank)—Unknown or not specified

a—Preschool

b—Primary

c—Elementary and junior high school

d—Secondary (senior high school)

e—Adult

f—Specialized

g—General

j—Juvenile

23–27 Accompanying matter. Up to five character codes (recorded in alphabetical order) that indicate the type of production and publicity material that accompanies, primarily, an archival motion picture. If fewer than five codes are assigned, the codes are left-justified and each unused position contains a blank.

(blank)—No accompanying matter

l—Stills

m—Script material

o—Posters

p—Pressbooks

q—Lobby cards

r—Instructional materials

s—Music. A musical score or other music format.

z—Other

28 Government publication. A one-character code indicating whether the item is published or produced by or for a government agency, and if so, the jurisdictional level of the agency.

(blank)—Not a government publication

a—Autonomous or semi-autonomous component

c—Multilocal

f—Federal/national

i—International/intergovernmental

l—Local

m—Multistate

o—Government publication—level undetermined

s—State, provincial, territorial, dependent, etc.

u—Unknown if item is government publication or not

z—Other

29–32 Undefined. Each contains a blank (.) or fill character (l).

33 Type of visual material.

a—Art original

b—Kit

c—Art reproduction

d—Diorama

f—Filmstrip

g—Game

i—Picture

k—Graphic

l—Technical drawing

m—Motion picture

n—Chart

o—Flash card

p—Microscope slide

q—Model

r—Realia

s—Slide

t—Transparency

v—Videorecording

w—Toy

z—Other

34 Technique.

a—Animation

c—Animation and live action

l—Live action

n—Not applicable. Item is not a motion picture or a videorecording.

u—Unknown

z—Other technique

35–37 Language. A three-character code indicating the language of the item.

38 Modified record. A one-character code that indicates whether any data in a bibliographic record is a modification of information that appeared on the item being cataloged or that was intended to be included in the USMARC record. Codes are assigned a priority, and, when more than one code applies to the item, are recorded in the order of the following list.

(blank)—Not modified.

d—Dashed-on information.

o—Completely romanized/printed in script.

s—Shortened. Some data omitted because the record would have exceeded the maximum length allowed by a particular system.

x—Missing characters. Characters could not be converted into machine-readable form due to character set limitations.

39   Cataloging source. A one-character code that indicates the creator of the original cataloging record. The National Union Catalog (NUC) symbol or the name of the organization may be contained in subfield ≠a of field 040.

(blank)—Library of Congress

a—National Agricultural Library

b—National Library of Medicine

c—Library of Congress cooperative cataloging program

d—Other sources [most libraries fall here]

n—Report to *New Serial Titles*

u—Unknown

Videorecordings, 008 (Header) Information Exercises

2.4.1. Running time

a.   _____ 25 minutes

b.   _____ 2 hours

c.   _____ 10 1/2 minutes

d.   _____ 20 hours

e.   _____ About 25 minutes

2.4.2. Target audience

a.   _____ Junior high school

b.   _____ Kindergarten

c.   _____ Adult

d.   _____ All ages

e.   _____ Preschool

f.   _____ Senior high

g.   _____ Specialized audience

h.   _____ Juvenile

i.   _____ Second grade

2.4.3. Accompanying matter

a.   _____ Music, lobby cards, and posters

b.   _____ Stills, instructional materials

c.   _____ Instructional materials, script material, historical information

d.   _____ None

e.   _____ Biographical information, pressbooks

2.4.4. Government publications

a.   ____ Local

b.   ____ Federal

c.   ____ State

d.   ____ International

e.   ____ Not governmental

f.   ____ Multilocal

g.   ____ Multistate

2.4.5. Type of visual material

a.   ____ Flash card

b.   ____ Filmstrip

c.   ____ Toy

d.   ____ Game

e.   ____ Motion picture

f.   ____ Technical drawing

g.   ____ Art original

h.   ____ Transparency

2.4.6. Technique

a.   ____ Live action

b.   ____ Unknown

c.   ____ Claymation

d.   ____ Animation

e.   ____ Computer enhanced graphics

Fill in the 008 field with the correct codes.

2.4.7.   008   . . . .

245 00   ≠a African exodus ≠h [videorecording] : ≠b the origins of modern humanity.

260   ≠a New York :≠b Windy Video, ≠c c1996.

300   ≠a 1 videocassette (23 min.) : ≠b sd., col. ; ≠c 1/2 in.

500   ≠a Based on the book of the same title.

538   ≠a VHS format.

520   ≠a Filmed in Africa, this lovely production gives the history of man's diffusion throughout the rest of the world.

700 1   ≠a Stringer, Chris.

2.4.8.   008 . . . .

245 04   ≠a The seeing glass ≠h [videorecording] : ≠b a memoir.

260   ≠a New York : ≠b Riverhead Video, ≠c p1997.

300   ≠a 1 videocassette (56 min.) : ≠b sd., col. ; ≠c 1/2 in.

520   ≠a Jacquelin Gorman tells in interviews, still pictures, and historical footage, the story of her life.

600 10   ≠a Gorman, Jacquelin.

700 1   ≠a Gorman, Jacquelin.

2.4.9.   008 . . . .

245 04   ≠a The new Americans ≠h [videorecording] : ≠b how immigrants renew our country.

260   ≠a Starkville, Miss. : ≠b University of Mississippi, ≠c p1994.

300   ≠a 1 videocassette (42 min.) : ≠b sd., b&w ; ≠c 1/2 in. + ≠e 1 teacher's guide.

500   ≠a Based on the book by Jackie Stillman.

538   ≠a VHS format.

521   ≠a "Intended for high school social science classes."--container.

520   ≠a The story of immigrants to America. Includes historical footage and stills from Ellis Island, New York, Chicago, and more.

700 1   ≠a Stillman, Jackie.

2.4.10. 008 . . . .

245 00   ≠a Declaration of Independence, the American scripture ≠h [videorecording].

260   ≠a New York : ≠b Windy Video, ≠c p1995.

300   ≠a 1 videocassette (51 min.) : ≠b sd., col. ; ≠c 1/2 in.

440 0   ≠a Historical documents series

500   ≠a Based on the book by Sharon Meyer.

500   ≠a Closed captioned for the hearing impaired.

538   ≠a VHS format.

521   ≠a "Grades 4-8"--Container.

700 1   ≠a Meyer, Sharon.

2.4.11. 008 . . . .

245 00   ≠a History of America's murders ≠h [videorecording].

260   ≠a Columbus, Ohio : ≠b Field Video, ≠c c1996.

300   ≠a 1 videocassette (30 min.) : ≠b sd., col./b&w ; ≠c 1/2 in.

500   ≠a Based on the book by Elaine Rogers.

520   ≠a Shows the documents and photographs in some of America's most tragic murders. Warning: includes some very graphic still shots which may be offensive to some persons.

700 1   ≠a Rogers, Elaine.

2.4.12. 008 . . . .

245 02   ≠a L'histoire de la Louisiane ≠h [videorecording].

250   ≠a 2nd ed.

260   ≠a Paris : ≠b L'editions Francaise, ≠c 1997.

300   ≠a 1 videocassette (93 min.) : ≠b sd., col. ; ≠c 1/2 in.

500   ≠a Commentary is in French.

511   ≠a Stars Genevieve Doucet as host.

520   ≠a Gives the history of Louisiana from its early exploration to the beginning of the twentieth century. Uses actors in authentic costumes and was filmed in contemporary settings.

651 0   ≠a Louisiana ≠x History ≠x Study and teaching (Elementary)

700   ≠a Doucet, Genevieve.

2.4.13. 008 . . . .

245 00   ≠a Dinosaurs ≠h [videorecording] : ≠b everything too aged.

250   ≠a 6th ed.

260   ≠a Provo, Utah : ≠b Mormon Video, ≠c 1993.

300   ≠a 1 videocassette (43 min.) : ≠b sd., col. ; ≠c 1/2 in.

511   ≠a Hosted by Billy Carter and Ronald Reagan.

520   ≠a A spoof on the American tendency to think of old things as worthless.

700 1   ≠a Reagan, Ronald.

700 1   ≠a Carter, Billy.

2.4.14.   008 . . . .

100 1   ≠a Aarons, Lettie.

245 10   ≠a Ballad of true love ≠h [videorecording] : ≠b love is blind, etc. / ≠c Lettie Aarons.

250   ≠a 2nd ed.

260   ≠a Chicago : ≠b Field Museum Press, ≠c 1997.

300   ≠a 1 videocassette (30 min.) : ≠b sd., col. ; ≠c 1/2 in.

500   ≠a Closed captioned for the hearing impaired.

538   ≠a VHS format.

520   ≠a Originally taped as a tribute to her children, there were so many requests for this beautiful item that it is now available to all.

2.5. Videorecordings, *AACR2R* Chapter 7 Exercises

The rules in chapter 7 of *AACR2R* cover the description of motion pictures and videorecordings. Because most libraries acquire more videorecordings than motion pictures, this workbook concentrates on videos. Motion picture examples and tagging are found in the chapter on miscellaneous formats. Note that the rules for 16mm motion pictures are the same as for videos, with the exception of the GMD and the SMDs.

Use Chapter 7 of *AACR2R* to answer the following questions about videorecordings.

2.5.1.   What is the chief source of information for videorecordings?

2.5.2.   What do you do if the videorecording lacks a title?

2.5.3.   Where do you put the GMD when a parallel title is involved?

2.5.4.   What do you do with a videorecording that lacks a collective title?

2.5.5.   Are you allowed to give the distributor of a videorecording in the imprint field?

2.5.6.   If the name of the manufacturer is different from that of the publisher, do you give it as well in the imprint field?

2.5.7.   How do you designate playing time of a videodisc consisting of still images?

2.5.8.   When do you give the projection speed of a film in frames per second?

2.5.9.   If the videorecording has an ISBN (International Standard Book Number), do you use it even though the item is not a book?

2.5.10.   Where does information on videorecordings come from if the chief source has none? (Usually this would be unpublished material; most published videorecordings contain at least the title on the item, or on the container.)

2.5.11.   Where does the information on unedited material and newsfilm come from?

2.5.12.   How do you designate the item if it is a trailer containing extracts from a larger film?

2.5.13.   Where do you put the information that a videorecording is a colorized version of an older motion picture?

2.5.14.   How do you note the difference between a publisher, distributor, or releasing agency?

2.5.15.   What are the specific material designations (SMDs) used with videorecordings?

2.5.16.   What "other physical details" are given in the physical details field, ≠b (the second subfield)?

2.5.17.   Do you use millimeters or inches to give the size of a videorecording?

2.5.18.   Which rule gives prescribed punctuation for videorecordings?

2.5.19.   Where is the general material designation (GMD) placed?

2.5.20.   What information goes in the statement of responsibility for a videorecording?

2.5.21.   If you are cataloging a foreign film, how do you transcribe the edition statement?

2.5.22.   In the imprint statement, do you use the date of the original production or the date of the print you are cataloging?

2.5.23.   Do you give the trade name of a recording system (VHS, SECAM) as a specification in the physical description field?

2.5.24.   How do you designate a silent film?

2.5.25.   Is transcription of series statements different for videorecordings?

2.5.26.   How does the user know if the title proper is not taken from the chief source of information?

2.5.27.   When would you use the GMD [kit]?

2.5.28.   Do you use both names in the statement of responsibility if one agency produces an item for another agency?

2.5.29.   Which area is *not* used for motion pictures and videorecordings?

2.5.30.   What date do you give in the imprint field for an unedited or unpublished videocassette (such as a home movie)?

2.5.31.   Where do you indicate the playing time of a videorecording?

2.5.32.   How do you indicate the color of a videorecording in a sepia print?

2.5.33.   Give the order of notes for videorecordings.

3.

SOUND RECORDINGS

Sound recordings come in different formats—they may be disks, either compact disc or long-play disk; cassettes; or tape reels. The physical description field is important here to indicate which format is being cataloged.

Sound recordings, unlike videorecordings, are not always entered under title main entry. Some classical works are entered under composer, others under performer. Most popular music recordings will be entered under performer. Audiobooks use the same main entry as the printed book. When there is more than one possible main entry, it is especially important to use *AACR2R* to determine the correct access point and the correct manner of recording the name.

Audiobooks usually contain a summary and subject headings. These will greatly assist the user in determining if the item is of interest. Other details, such as the presence of graphic language, violence, and death, are usually noted as well. The audience level should be included if it is readily ascertainable.

3.1. Sound Recordings, Full Records Tagging Exercises

3.1.1. 100 _   ____ O'Connor, Tony.

245 _ _   ____ Uluru ____ [sound recording] / ____ Tony O'Connor.

260   ____ Nambour, Qld., Australia : ____ Studio Horizon Productions, ____ [c1992].

300   ____ 1 sound disc : ____ digital, stereo. ; ____ 4 3/4 in.

505 _   ____ Freedom -- Valley of winds -- Mutitjula walk -- Dune -- Above with eagles -- Desert oak -- Touching sky -- Uluru.

511   ____ Tony O'Connor, Paul Clement, Marshal Whyler.

508   ____ Composed, arranged, and performed by Tony O'Connor ; production and direction by Jackie O'Connor.

650 _   ____ Popular music ____ Australia.

3.1.2. 100 _ ____ Kershaw, Doug.

245 _ _ ____ The best of south Louisiana ____ [sound recording] / ____ Doug Kershaw and his band.

260 ____ Baton Rouge, La. : ____ Roll 'Em Productions, ____ 1962.

300 ____ 1 sound disc (80 min.) : ____ digital, stereo. ; ____ 4 3/4 in.

500 ____ Compact disc.

650 _ ____ Popular music ____ Louisiana.

3.1.3. 1_ _ ____ McCaffrey, Anne.

2_ _ _ ____ Acorna, the unicorn girl ____ [sound recording] / ____ Anne McCaffrey and Margaret Ball.

2_ ____ New York : ____ Harper Audiobooks, ____ c1997.

3_ ____ 13 sound recordings (19.5 hrs.) : ____ mono.

5_ ____ Unabridged.

5_ ____ Read by Sandra McIntyre-Colby.

5_ ____ When three miners find an escape pod with a live unicorn girl inside, they decide to adopt her and raise her themselves instead of letting her be mutilated and imprisoned by ambitious scientists.

6_ _ ____ Fantastic fiction. ____ gsafd

7_ _ ____ Ball, Margaret.

7_ _ ____ McIntyre-Colby, Sandra.

3.1.4. 1_ _ ____ Carter, Hodding, ____ 1907-1972.

2_ _ _ ____ John Law wasn't so wrong ____ [sound recording] / ____ by Hodding Carter.

2_ ____ 1st ed.

2_ ____ Baton Rouge, La. : ____ Esso Standard Oil Co., ____ c1952.

3_ ____ 1 sound disk (20 min.) : ____ 33 1/3 rpm, mono. ; ____ 12 in.

5_ ____ Narrated by Edwin Edwards.

6_ _ ____ Louisiana ____ Economic conditions.

6_ _ ____ Louisiana ____ Industries.

7_ _ ____ Edwards, Edwin W.

3.1.5. 1__ _   ____ Wilds, John.

2__ _ _   ____ Alton Ochsner, surgeon of the South ____ [sound recording] / ____ John Wilds and Ira Harkey.

2__   ____ Baton Rouge : ____ Louisiana State University Press, ____ 1990.

3__   ____ 2 sound cassettes (120 min.) : ____ mono.

5__   ____ Read by Ira Harkey.

6__ _ _   ____ Ochsner, Alton, ____ 1896-

6__ _   ____ Surgeons ____ Louisiana ____ Biography.

7__ _   ____ Harkey, Ira, ____ 1918-

3.1.6. 1__ _   ____ Lynn, Stuart M.

2__ _ _   ____ New Orleans ____ [sound recording] / ____ by Stuart M. Lynn.

2__   ____ New York : ____ Hastings House Audio, ____ 1949.

3__   ____ 1 sound disk (68 min.) : ____ mono.

5__   ____ Read by Julie Aillet.

5__   ____ A tour of New Orleans giving historical information about various places in the Vieux Carré, or French Quarter, of New Orleans, Louisiana.

6__ _   ____ Vieux Carré (New Orleans, La.) ____ Description and travel.

6__ _   ____ New Orleans (La.) ____ History.

7__ _   ____ Aillet, Julie.

3.1.7. __ _ _   ____ By hand and by eye ____ [sound recording] : ____ South Louisiana wooden boat builders and their stories / ____ Center for Traditional Louisiana Boatbuilding, Nicholls State University.

___   ____ Thibodaux, La. : ____ The Center, ____ 1986.

___   ____ 2 sound cassettes (120 min.) : ____ mono.

___ _   ____ Boat building oral history series

___   ____ Four boatbuilders from south Louisiana tell the way they got into the boat building business and how each learned his trade.

___ _   ____ Boatbuilding ____ Louisiana.

___ _   ____ Louisiana ____ History, Local.

___ _   ____ Oral history.

___ _   ____ Nicholls State University. ____ Center for Traditional Louisiana Boatbuilding.

This one is all yours—no help, no tips, no blanks. Good luck.

3.1.8. ___ _   Connolly, John B.

___ _ _   Underway [sound recording] : tour of a tin can sailor / John B. Connolly.

___ _ _   Tour of a tin can sailor.

___   Baton Rouge, La. : J.B. Connolly, 1990.

___   2 sound cassettes (150 min.) : mono.

___   Sold by subscription to raise money for the Veterans of Foreign Wars.

___   Read by the author, this cassette package gives the memoirs of J.B. Connolly's tour of duty as a member of the U.S. Navy during the Korean War.

___ _ _   Connolly, John B.

___ _ _   United States. Navy Biography.

___ _   Korean War, 1950-1953 Personal narratives, American.

3.2. Sound Recordings, Notes Exercise

Read section 6.7 in *Anglo-American Cataloguing Rules*, 2nd edition, 1988 revision. Use the order given there to put the notes in the bibliographic record shown here in the correct order. Number the notes from 1 to 10 on the blanks. The projected title is given in bold letters at the top of the set of notes.

Christmas in the Holy Land

____   Performed in Arabic, English, French, and Latin.

____   Title on dust jacket: Jerusalem at Christmas.

____   With: Requiem mass.

____   Title from disc label.

____   Distributed in the United States by Columbia Records.

____   Intended audience: All ages.

____   Columbia records: CRS-1431.

____   Compact disc.

____   English translation of carols and Requiem mass on container.

____   Carols and mass recorded in Jerusalem.

3.3. Sound Recordings, Error Identification Exercises

The number of errors in each record is given in parentheses at the top of the record. Find the errors and circle them. Write the corrections above the errors. The errors may be in spelling, tags, indicators, subfields, punctuation, etc.

3.3.1. (20 errors)

100 1   ≠a Rodgers, Richard, ≠y 1902-

130 04   ≠a The sound of music. ≠h [sound recording]

245 14   ≠a Mary Martin in The sound of music. ≠h [sound recording] : ≠c music by

Richard Rodgers ; lyrics by Oscar Hammerstein, 2nd.

301   New York : ≠b Columbia, ≠c p1959.

300   ≠a 1 sound recording : ≠b analog, 33 1/3 rpm, stereo. ; ≠c 11 in.

511   ≠a Mary Martin, Theodore Bikel, and the original stge cast.

505   ≠A Based on the book "The Trapp Family Singers" by Maria Augusta Trapp.

651 0   ≠a Motion picture music.

740 02   ≠a Hammerstein, Richard, ≠c 1895-1960.

740 41   ≠a The sound of music.

3.3.2. (12 errors)

100 1   ≠a The Oak Ridge Boys ≠q (Musical group)

245 14   ≠a The Oka Ridge Boys have arrived [sound recording] / $c The Oak Ridge

Boys.

260 0   ≠a [Los Angeles, CA] : ≠b ABC Records, ≠d (manufactured and distributed

by CRT of Canada); ≠c c1979.

300   ≠a 1 audiocassette (33 min.) : ≠b stereo.

511   ≠a Produced by Ron Chancey ; string and horn arrangements by Bergen White.

650 0   Popular music, Country style.

3.3.3. (24 errors)

100 20   ≠a Shostakovich, Dmitrii Dmitrievich, ≠a 1906-1975.

240 14   ≠a Concertos, ≠a violoncello, orchestra, ≠n no. 1, op. 107, ≠r E♭.

245 10   ≠t Concertoe for cello, in E flat, op. 107. ≠a Symphony no. 1, in F major,

op. 10 [sound recording] / Shostakovitch.

260   ≠a New York City, New York : ≠b Columbia, ≠c [1960?]

300   ≠a 1 sound disc (57 min.) ; ≠c digital, stereo. 4 3/4 in.

410 0   ≠a Columbia masterworks.

508   ≠a Mstislav Rostropovich, violonchello ; Mason Jones, French horn ; The

Philadelphia Orcestra, Eugene Ormandy, conductor.

500   ≠a Program notes on container.

650 0   ≠t Symphonies.

650 0   ≠a Violoncello concertos

740 02   ≠a Shostakovich, Dmitrii D., ≠d 1906-1975. ≠x Symphonies, ≠n no. 1,

op. 10, ≠r F major.

3.3.4. (8 errors)

110 1   ≠a Captian & Tennille (Music group)

245 10   ≠a Love will keep us together ≠h sound cassette / ≠a The Captain & Tennille.

260   ≠a Beverley Hills, Calif. : ≠b A&M Records, ≠c 1975.

300   ≠a 1 sound disk (ca. 35 min.) : ≠b 33 1/3 rpm, stereo. ; ≠c 3 7/8 × 2 1/2 in.

650 0   ≠a Music, Popular (Songs, etc.) ≠z United States.

3.3.5. (1 error)

100 1   ≠a Mantovani, Annunzio Paolo, ≠d 1905-

245 10   ≠a Merry Christmas with Mantovani ≠h [sound recording].

246 10   ≠a Christmas greetings from Mantovani and his orchestra.

260   ≠a [New York] : ≠b London, ≠c [1970?]

300   ≠a 1 sound disk (60.5 min.) : ≠b 33 1/3 rpm, stereo. ; ≠c 12 in.

500   ≠a Title on container: Christmas greetings from Mantovani and his orchestra.

650 0   ≠a Carols (Instrumental settings)

650 0   ≠a Christmas music.

3.3.6. (16 errors)

245 00   ≠a Fox's book of marters / \c edited by William B. Forbush.

262   ≠a Nashville, N.Y. : ≠b Zondervan, ≠c c1967, c1968, c1969.

300   ≠a 1 sound cassettes (15 hrs.) : ≠b mono.

511   ≠n Read by Sir Robert Burns.

650 0   ≠a Persocution ≠x Moral and ethical aspects.

650 0   ≠a Saints ≠z Biography.

650 0   ≠a Martyrs ≠z Biography.

700 2   ≠a Forbush, William Byron, ≠c 1868-1927.

720 1   ≠a Burns, Robert, Sir.

3.3.7. (12 errors)

100 1   ≠a Urbenski, Verna.

245 04   ≠a Cataloging unpublished nonprint materials ≠h audio cassette / ≠c by Verna Urbanski, principal author, with Bao Chu Chang and Bernard L. Karon ; edited by Edward Svenson.

250   ≠a First edition.

260   ≠a Lake Crystal, Minn. : ≠b Solder Creek Press, ≠c 1992.

300   ≠a 1 sound recording (120 hrs.)

508   ≠a Read by the author.

650 0   ≠a Cataloging of nonprint materials.

650 0   ≠a Anglo-American cataloging rules.

3.3.8. (10 errors)

100 10   ≠a Paul Newman.

245 04   ≠a The sting ≠a [sound recording] / ≠c Universal Pictures.

260   ≠a University City, CA : ≠b Universal Pictures, ≠c 1988.

300   ≠a 1 sound disc (60 min.) : ≠b stereo. ; ≠c 3 7/8 in.

501   ≠a Music from the motion picture by the same title.

508   ≠a Robert Redford, Roert Shaw, Paul Newman.

700 21   ≠a Redford, Robert.

700 21   ≠a Shawm, Robert.

3.4. Sound Recordings, 008 (Header) Information

The codes given here are specifically for sound recordings. Use them to create 008 fields for the records in the exercises following the code list.

00–05   Date entered on file; indicates the date the record was created; recorded in the pattern *yymmdd* (year/year/month/month/day/day).

06   Type of date/publication status. One-character code that categorizes the type of dates given in 008/07–10 (Date 1) and 008/11–14 (Date 2). For serials, 008/06 also indicates the publication status.

   (blank)—No dates given; B.C. date involved. Each character in fields 008/07–10 and 008/11–14 contains a blank.

   c—Serial item currently published. 008/07–10 contains the beginning date of publication; 008/11–14 contains 9999.

   d—Serial item ceased publication. 008/07–10 contains beginning date of publication; 008/11–14 contains ending date.

   e—Detailed date; 008/07–10 contains year and 008/11–14 contains month and day, recorded as *mmdd*.

   i—Inclusive dates of collection.

   k—Range of years of bulk of collection.

   m—Multiple dates; 008/07–10 usually contains the beginning date and 008/11–14 contains the ending date.

   n—Dates unknown; each position in 008/07–10 and 008/11–14 contains blanks.

   p—Date of distribution/release/issue and production/recording session when different.

   q—Questionable date; 008/07–10 contains the earliest possible date; 008/11–14 contains the latest possible date.

   r—Reprint/reissue date and original date; 008/07–10 contains the date of reproduction or reissue (i.e., the most current date) and 008/11–14 contains the date of the original, if known.

   s—Single known/probable date. 008/07–10 contains the date; 008/11–14 contains blanks.

   t—Publication date and copyright date.

   u—Serial status unknown. 008/07–10 contains the beginning date of publication; 008/11–14 contains 9999.

07-10   (Date 1)

   (blank)—Date element is not applicable.

   u—Date element is totally or partially unknown.

11-14   (Date 2)

>   (blank)—Date element is not applicable.

>   u—Date element is totally or partially unknown.

15–17   Place of publication, production, or execution. A two- or three-character code that indicates the place of publication, production, or execution. Two-character codes are left-justified and the unused position contains a blank (.). [Codes for the United States consist of the two-letter ZIP code abbreviation plus *u* for United States. New York, for example, would be coded *nyu*.] Unless otherwise specified, codes are always lower-case letters.

18–19   Form of composition. A two-character code that indicates the form of composition of printed or manuscript music or a musical sound recording. If more than one code is appropriate, the code *mu* (Multiple forms) is used in 008/18–19 and all appropriate specific codes are given in field 047 (Form of Composition).

>   an—Anthems
>   bg—Bluegrass music
>   bl—Blues
>   bt—Ballets
>   ca—Chaconnes
>   cb—Chants, Other religions
>   cc—Chant, Christian
>   cg—Concerti grossi
>   ch—Chorales
>   cl—Chorale preludes
>   cn—Canons and rounds
>   co—Concertos
>   cp—Chansons, polyphonic
>   cr—Carols
>   cs—Chance compositions
>   ct—Cantatas
>   cy—Country music
>   cz—Canzonas
>   df—Dance forms (other than mazurkas, minuets, pavans, polonaises, and waltzes)
>   dv—Divertimentos, serenades, cassations, divertissements, notturni
>   fg—Fugues
>   fm—Folk music
>   ft—Fantasias
>   gm—Gospel music
>   hy—Hymns
>   jz—Jazz

mc—Musical revues and comedies

md—Madrigals

mi—Minuets

mo—Motets

mp—Motion picture music

mr—Marches

ms—Masses

mu—Multiple forms

mz—Mazurkas

nc—Nocturnes

nn—Not applicable

op—Operas

or—Oratorios

ov—Overtures

pg—Program music

pm—Passion music

po—Polonaises

pp—Popular music

pr—Preludes

ps—Passacaglias

pt—Part songs

pv—Pavans

rc—Rock music

rd—Rondos

rg—Ragtime music

ri—Ricercars

rq—Requiems

sg—Songs

sn—Sonatas

sp—Symphonic poems

st—Studies and exercises

su—Suites

sy—Symphonies

tc—Toccatas

ts—Trio-sonatas

uu—Unknown

vr—Variations

wz—Waltzes

zz—Other

20   Format of music. A one-character code that indicates the format of a printed or manuscript music composition.

       a—Full score

       b—Full score, miniature or study size

       c—Accompaniment reduced for keyboard

       d—Voice score

       e—Condensed score or piano-conductor score

       g—Close score

       m—Multiple score formats

       n—Not applicable

       u—Unknown

       z—Other

21   Undefined. Contains a blank (.) or fill character (|).

22   Target audience.

       (blank)—Unknown or not specified

       a—Preschool

       b—Primary

       c—Elementary and junior high school

       d—Secondary (senior high school)

       e—Adult

       f—Specialized

       g—General

       j—Juvenile

23   Form of item. The form of material for printed or manuscript music.

       (blank)—None of the following

       a—Microfilm

       b—Microfiche

       c—Microopaque

       d—Large print

       f—Braille

       r—Regular print reproduction (eye-readable print)

24–29   Accompanying matter. Up to six one-character codes recorded in alphabetical order that indicate the contents of program notes and other accompanying material. If fewer than six codes are assigned, the codes are left-justified and each unused position contains a blank.

       (blank)—No accompanying matter

       a—Discography

b—Bibliography

c—Thematic index

d—Libretto or text

e—Biography of composer or author

f—Biography of performer or history of ensemble

g—Technical and/or historical information on instruments

h—Technical information on music

i—Historical information

k—Ethnological information

r—Instructional materials

s—Music

z—Other

30–31   Literary text for sound recordings

(blank)—Item is a musical sound recording

a—Autobiography

b—Biography

c—Conference proceedings

d—Drama

e—Essays

f—Fiction

g—Reporting

h—History

i—Instruction

j—Language instruction

k—Comedy

l—Lectures, speeches

m—Memoirs

n—Not applicable

o—Folktales

p—Poetry

r—Rehearsals

s—Sounds

t—Interviews

z—Other

32–34   Undefined. Each contains a blank (.) or a fill character (l).

35–37   Language. A three-character code indicating the language of the item.

38   Modified record. A one-character code that indicates whether any data in a bibliographic record is a modification of information that appeared on the item being cataloged or that was intended to be included in the USMARC record. Codes are assigned a priority, and, when more than one code applies to the item, are recorded in the order of the following list.

(blank)—Not modified.

d—Dashed-on information.

o—Completely romanized/printed in script.

s—Shortened. Some data omitted because the record would have exceeded the maximum length allowed by a particular system.

x—Missing characters. Characters could not be converted into machine-readable form due to character set limitations.

39   Cataloging source. A one-character code that indicates the creator of the original cataloging record. The NUC symbol or the name of the organization may be contained in subfield ≠a of field 040.

(blank)—Library of Congress

a—National Agricultural Library

b—National Library of Medicine

c—Library of Congress cooperative cataloging program

d—Other sources [most libraries fall here]

n—Report to *New Serial Titles*

u—Unknown

Sound Recordings, 008 (Header) Information Exercises

3.4.1. Form of composition

a   _____ Concertos

b.   _____ Mazurkas

c.   _____ Ricercars

d.   _____ Symphonies

e.   _____ Unknown

f.   _____ Preludes

g.   _____ Jazz and hymns

h.   _____ Part-songs

i.   _____ Dance forms

j.   _____ Sonatas

3.4.2. Format of music

a.   _____ Miniature full score

b.   _____ Close score

c.   _____ Vocal score

d.   _____ Full score

e. ____ Multiple score formats

f. ____ Piano-conductor score

g. ____ Keyboard accompaniment

h. ____ Unknown

i. ____ Study size

3.4.3. Target audience

a. ____ Third grade

b. ____ Preschool

c. ____ Adult

d. ____ General

e. ____ Junior high

3.4.4. Form of item

a. ____ Microfilm

b. ____ Microopaque

c. ____ Large print

d. ____ Microfiche

e. ____ Braille

f. ____ Eye-readable

g. ____ Not applicable

3.4.5. Accompanying matter

a. ____ Bibliography, biographies of composer and performers

b. ____ Thematic index, libretto, music, historical information

c. ____ Technical information on instruments and on music

d. ____ Discography, libretto, biography of composer

e. ____ Thematic index

f. ____ Historical information, technical information on instruments, ethnological information, instructional materials

g. ____ Discography, bibliography, libretto

3.4.6. Literary text

a. ____ Biography

b. ____ Essays

c. ____ Conference proceedings

d. ____ Autobiography

e. ____ Fiction

f. ____ Memoirs

g. ____ Interviews

h. ____ Folktales

i. ____ Lectures, speeches

Fill in the 008 field with the correct codes.

3.4.7. 008   . . . .

100 1   ≠a Stringer, Chris.

245 00   ≠a African exodus ≠h [sound recording] : ≠b the origins of modern humanity.

260   ≠a New York :≠b Windy Video, ≠c c1996.

300   ≠a 1 sound cassette (26 min.) : ≠b mono.

500   ≠a Based on the book of the same title, excerpted and read by the author.

520   ≠a Tells the history of man's diffusion throughout the rest of the world.

3.4.8. 008   . . . .

245 00   ≠a Dinosaurs ≠h [sound recording] : ≠b everything too aged.

250   ≠a 6th ed.

260   ≠a Provo, Utah : ≠b Mormon Audio, ≠c 1993.

300   ≠a 1 sound cassette (43 min.) : ≠b mono.

511   ≠a Hosted by Billy Carter and Ronald Reagan.

520   ≠a A spoof on the American tendency to think of old things as worthless.

700 1   ≠a Reagan, Ronald.

700 1   ≠a Carter, Billy.

3.4.9. 008   . . . .

100 1   ≠a Aarons, Lettie.

245 10   ≠a Ballad of true love ≠h [sound recording] : ≠b love is blind.

250   ≠a 2nd ed.

260   ≠a Chicago : ≠b Windy Press Audio, ≠c p1997.

300   ≠a 1 sound cassette (35 min.) : ≠b stereo.

520   ≠a Vignettes of love from childhood to the elderly, including parents and grandparents, husband and wife, and friends.

3.4.10. 008   . . . .

100 1   ≠a DeKing, Elizabeth.

245 00   ≠a Cry for me, my darlings ≠h [sound recording].

260   ≠a London : ≠b Chidi Press, ≠c p1997.

300   ≠a 1 sound cassette (52 min.)

500   ≠a Excerpts from the novel by Elizabeth DeKing.

520   ≠a Many families lost everything in the great fire of London in the nineteenth century. This is the story of one family's life after the fire.

3.4.11.   008   . . . .

245 00   ≠a Rage for age ≠h [sound recording] : ≠b the increasing elder generation.

250   ≠a 1st ed.

260   ≠a Washington D.C. : ≠b Dept. of Health, Education, and Welfare ; for sale by the U.S. G.P.O., ≠c 1997.

300   ≠a 1 sound cassette (26 min.)

511   ≠a Narrated by George Bush.

520   ≠a The baby boomers are getting older, and society is going to have to cope with the increased costs and influences of an aging population.

3.4.12.   008   . . . .

245 00   ≠a Beer for all! ≠h [sound recording] : ≠b and other campaign promises not kept.

260   ≠a Kansas City, MO : ≠b Beer Industry League, ≠c p1996.

300   ≠a 1 sound cassette (58 min.)

500   ≠a Based on the book by Phillips Van Heusen.

500   ≠a Narrated by Phillips Van Heusen.

521   ≠a "Intended for use in high school civics classes."--container.

520   ≠a Uses excerpts from campaign speeches to show how politicians don't always keep the promises they make when campaigning.

700 1   ≠a Van Heusen, Phillips.

3.4.13.   008   . . . .

100 1   ≠a Wilder, Genevieve.

245 10   ≠a Mothers know best ≠h [sound recording].

260   ≠a Good Living, AK : ≠b Snow School Press, ≠c 1997.

300   ≠a 1 sound cassette (30 min.)

500   ≠a Created by the mothers of Snow School in Good Living, Alaska, to show good skiing practices and safety habits.

3.4.14.   008   . . . .

100 1   ≠a Hines, Earl, ≠d 1905-

245 10   ≠a My tribute to Louis ≠h [sound recording] : ≠b piano solos / ≠c by Earl Hines.

260   ≠a [S.l.] : ≠b Audiophile, ≠c [1971?]

300   ≠a 1 sound disc (ca. 50 min.) : ≠b analog, 33 1/3 rpm, stereo. ; ≠c 12 in.

505 0   ≠a When it's sleepy time down South -- Struttin' with some barbecue -- A kiss to build a dream on -- Pennies from Heaven -- Confessin' -- Muskrat ramble -- Blueberry Hill -- Someday you'll be sorry -- When it's sleepy time down South.

3.5. Sound Recordings, *AACR2R* Chapter 6 Exercises

3.5.1.   What formats of sound recordings do the rules in Chapter 6 cover?

3.5.2.   What does Chapter 6 *not* cover?

3.5.3.   What types of responsibilities are transcribed in the 245 ǂc?

3.5.4.   If you are describing a sound recording containing separate parts as a unit, which *AACR2R* rule tells you how to construct the titles?

3.5.5.   If you are in doubt as to whether a name is a publishing subdivision or a series name, what do you do?

3.5.6.   If the item being cataloged has several separately titled parts, and you are cataloging one part of this item on a separate bibliographic record, how do you code the extent of the item (300 ǂa)?

3.5.7.   How do you record the size of a multipart item if the parts differ in size?

3.5.8.   Do you give the ISBN or ISSN, even if the item is not a book?

3.5.9.   When do you treat accompanying textual material or a container as the chief source of information for a sound recording?

3.5.10.   In which field do you give the statement of responsibility when the participation is confined to performance, execution, or interpretation?

3.5.11.   If you are in doubt about whether the item you're cataloging is a different edition, what should you do?

3.5.12.   Where do you record the date of recording, which is different from the date of publication?

3.5.13.   Give the order of the details for the second subfield of the physical description field (other physical details).

3.5.14.   What is the standard size and tape width of sound cassettes?

3.5.15.   What is the general material designation (GMD) for sound recordings?

3.5.16.   When would you give credit to individual performers as well as to the group to which they belong, and where would they be listed?

3.5.17.   How does *AACR2R* define "nonprocessed sound recording"?

3.5.18.   Where is the date of recording of a nonprocessed sound recording put?

3.5.19.   If the playing speed is standard for the type of item being cataloged, is it recorded in the physical description field?

3.5.20.   What dimensions do you give for a piano roll?

3.5.21.   Where is the GMD placed in a bibliographic record?

3.5.22.   How should items without a collective title be described in a bibliographic record?

3.5.23.   If a sound recording contains both the name of a publisher and the name of a subordinate unit of the company, which one is used in the imprint field?

3.5.24.   What are the specific material designations (SMDs) used with sound recordings?

3.5.25.   What are the terms used to describe the number of sound channels?

3.5.26.   What is the order of notes to be added to cataloging for sound recordings?

4.

COMPUTER FILES

Having to catalog computer files is the fear of nearly all catalogers, until they gain experience with the format. As this type of material comprises both data and computer programs, and is encoded for manipulation by computer, it may be found on floppy disks (both 3.5 and 5.25-inch disks), on CD-ROMs in optical form, and in electronic format housed at a remote site from the library cataloging it. This last category includes electronic journals and Internet sites.

As it is not always possible to actually load the software being cataloged, *AACR2R* allows the option of taking information from sources (container, label, or guide) other than the chief source, which is the projected title.

Main entry for software is under the name of the creator of the program, if it can be determined. Electronic media accessed through the Internet or other online services are not housed at the cataloging institution. The bibliographic record for such an item does not, therefore, have a physical details field—there is no physical object to describe.

Bibliographic records for electronic material must also contain information on accessing the title in question. For Internet sites, information such as the host site, the uniform resource locator (URL), and the date when the material was last updated are necessary parts of the bibliographic record.

Cataloging rules for multimedia items are still in their infancy. When one part of the item interacts with another part, linear progression and time length are sometimes not important. Notes are very important here—there are all sorts of information that are useful and must be included in the bibliographic record.

Don't panic! Experience will work wonders for your self-confidence.

4.1. Computer Files, Full Records Tagging Exercises

Add the proper tags, indicators, and subfields to the bibliographic records given here. The blanks indicate where tags, indicators, and subfields should be placed. Precede each subfield code with a delimiter. You will need to use the USMARC bibliographic formats, *AACR2R*, *LCSH*, and other tools.

4.1.1.   100 _   ____ Lutus, Paul.

245 _ _   ____ Musicomp ____ [computer file] / ____ by Paul Lutus.

246 _ _   ____ Music comp.

256   ____ Computer program (14 files)

260   ____ Cupertino, Calif. : ____ Apple Computer, Inc., ____ c1980.

300   ____ 1 computer disk : ____ sd., col. ; ____ 5 1/4 in. + ____ 1 manual (22 p. ; 22 cm.)

440 _   ____ Special delivery software

538   ____ System requirements: Apple II or higher.

520   ____ Uses the Apple's sound generating capability to play music and displays the musical notes on the screen as they are played. Also allows user to program his own compositions and add to the disk.

650 _   ____ Composition (Music)

650 _   ____ Music ____ Computer-assisted instruction.

710 _   ____ Apple Computer, Inc.

753   ____ Apple II

4.1.2.   100 _   ____ Williams, Robert.

245 _ _   ____ Missing facts ____ [computer file] / ____ by Robert Williams.

246 _ _   ____ Missing math facts.

260   ____ Freeport, N.Y. : ____ Educational Activities, ____ c1980.

300   ____ 1 computer disk : ____ col. ; ____ 5 1/4 in.

440 _   ____ Mathematics series

538   ____ System requirements: Apple II.

500   ____ Also called: Missing math facts.

500   ____ Copyright by Activity Records.

520   ____ Includes examples for addition, subtraction, multiplication, and division with four levels of difficulty for each process.

650 _   ____ Arithmetic ____ Computer-assisted instruction.

710 _   ____ Educational Activities (Firm)

710 _   ____ Activity Records Inc.

753   ____ Apple II

4.1.3.   1_ _   ____ Roos, T. B.

2_ _ _   ____ Life+ ____ [computer file] : ____ life, death, and change / ____ T.B. Roos.

2_ _ _   ____ Life, death, and change.

2_ _ _   ____ Life plus.

2_ _ _   ____ Biobits 1.

2_ _ _   ____ Biobits one.

2_ _ _   ____ Tribbles.

2_ _   ____ Wentworth, N.H. : ____ COMPress, ____ c1980.

3_   ____ 1 computer disk : ____ col. ; ____ 5 1/4 in. + ____ 1 manual and 1 Tribbles (student tutorial booklet).

5_   ____ System requirements: Apple IIe.

5_   ____ Title on guide: Biobits I: Life.

5_   ____ Tribbles: An introduction to the scientific method / Ruth Von Blum and Thomas Mercer Hursh.

5_   ____ Elements in a grid reproduce, maintain, or extinguish themselves according to a set of formal rules.

6_ _   ____ Science ____ Methodology.

7_ _   ____ Von Blum, Ruth.

7_ _   ____ Hursh, Thomas Mercer.

7_ _   ____ COMPress (Firm)

7_   ____ Apple IIe

4.1.4.   2_ _ _   ____ Microreporter ____ [computer file].

2_ _ _   ____ PC reporter.

2_   ____ Computer data (1 file : 800 records, 3150 bytes).

2_   ____ New York : ____ Simon & Schuster, ____ c1992.

3_   ____ 1 computer disk ; ____ 3 1/2 in.

5_   ____ System requirements: 386 system or higher; minimum 4 MB (8 MB recommended); Windows 3.0 or higher; hard drive; pen or stylus.

5_   ____ Title from title screen.

5_   ____ Title on disk label: PC reporter.

6_ _   ____ Journalism ____ Software.

7_   ____ IBM compatible

4.1.5.   1＿ ＿   ＿＿＿ Bergeron, Bryan P.

2＿ ＿ ＿   ＿＿＿ Heartlab ＿＿＿ [computer file] : ＿＿＿ clinical cardiology auscultatory simulation / ＿＿＿ [Bryan P. Bergeron].

2＿   ＿＿＿ Computer program.

2＿   ＿＿＿ [S.l.] : ＿＿＿ B.P. Bergeron, ＿＿＿ c1988.

3＿   ＿＿＿ 1 computer disk ; ＿＿＿ 3 1/2 in. + ＿＿＿ 1 guide (41 p.)

5＿   ＿＿＿ System requirements: Macintosh 512, 512E, Plus, SE, or Macintosh II; 512K; Heartblock sound interface; miniature stereo headphones.

5＿   ＿＿＿ Title from disk label.

5＿   ＿＿＿ "Developed in the Decision Systems Group, Brigham & Women's Hospital, Harvard Medical School"--Guide.

5＿   ＿＿＿ "Williams & Wilkins electronic media"--Guide.

6＿ ＿ ＿＿＿ Heart ＿＿＿ Study and teaching ＿＿＿ Software.

4.1.6.   2＿ ＿ ＿   ＿＿＿ Assessment of neuromotor dysfunction in infants ＿＿＿ [interactive multimedia] / ＿＿＿ produced by the Division of Developmental Disabilities, Dept. of Pediatrics, College of Medicine and Computer-Assisted Instruction Laboratory, Weeg Computing Center, the University of Iowa.

2＿   ＿＿＿ Baltimore : ＿＿＿ Williams & Wilkins, ＿＿＿ c1984.

3＿   ＿＿＿ 1 videodisc, 5 computer disks, 1 guide.

5＿   ＿＿＿ System requirements for videodisc: Pioneer LD-V6000 or compatible.

5＿   ＿＿＿ System requirements for computer disks: IBM PC or compatible; IBM InfoWindow System.

5＿   ＿＿＿ Title from cover of guide.

5＿   ＿＿＿ Title on videodisc label: Assessment of nevromotor [sic] dysfunction in infants.

5＿   ＿＿＿ Hosted by James A. Blackman, Loretta Knutson Lough, Joan Sustick Huntley.

5＿   ＿＿＿ Computer disks upgraded periodically.

5＿   ＿＿＿ "Williams & Wilkins electronic media"--Guide.

5＿ ＿   ＿＿＿ Assessment of neuromotor dysfunction in infants (version A) -- Pediatrics demo (automatic version) Pediatrics demo -- (non-automatic) -- Infant retrieval -- Assessment of neuromotor dysfunction in infants (version B).

6＿ ＿ ＿＿＿ Neurological disorders in infants ＿＿＿ Software.

7＿ ＿   ＿＿＿ University of Iowa. ＿＿＿ College of Pediatrics. ＿＿＿ Division of Developmental Disabilities.

4.1.7. ___ _ _   ____ Medication administration ____ [interactive multimedia] / ____ [American Journal of Nursing Company ; produced by Thomas Jefferson University, Office of Academic Computing and the Department of Nursing, College of Allied Health Sciences].

___   ____ [Philadelphia, Pa.] : ____ Thomas Jefferson University, ____ c1990-

___   ____ videodiscs : ____ sd., col. ; ____ 12 in.

___   ____ computer disks ; ____ 3 1/2–5 1/4 in.

___   ____ guides.

___   ____ System requirements for videodiscs: videodisc player.

___   ____ System requirements for computer disks: IBM PC or compatible; 640K (1 section requires 256K of graphics memory); DOS 3.3; InfoWindow Presentation System Interpreter, level 55; touch-screen monitor or M-Motion Video Adapter/A, EGA graphics display, 20MB hard disk.

___   ____ Title from t.p. of module 1 guide.

___   ____ Created by Sharon Renshaw, F. Scott Baedenkopf.

___   ____ Issued with full set of computer disks in both sizes.

___ _   ____ Pharmacopoeia ____ Software.

___ _   ____ Thomas Jefferson University. ____ Office of Academic Computing.

___ _   ____ Thomas Jefferson University. ____ Dept. of Nursing.

This one is all yours—no help, no tips, no blanks. Good luck.

4.1.8. ___ _ _   The American business disk [computer file].

___ _ _   Business for America.

___   Macintosh version.

___   Omaha, Neb. : J. Smith, c1992.

___   1 computer disk : col. ; 3 1/2 in. + 2 computer discs and guide.

___   System requirements: Macintosh System 7; VGA graphics card; 2 CD-ROM players.

___   Version information from disk label.

___   Title from title screen.

___   Title on CD-ROM disks: Business for America.

___ _   Business Software.

___   Macintosh System 7

4.2. Computer Files, Notes Exercises

Read section 9.7 in *Anglo-American Cataloguing Rules*, 2nd edition, 1988 revision. Use the order given there to put the notes in each bibliographic record here in the correct order. Number the notes from 1 to 10 on the blanks. The projected titles are given in bold letters at the top of the exercises.

Run to the White House

_____ Title on computer disk: Trail to the White House.

_____ Title from title screen.

_____ File size varies.

_____ Data collected by Alan Ferguson and Rick Acker.

_____ System requirements: IBM 486 or higher; DOS 6.1 or later; CD-ROM disk drive and controller card.

_____ Primarily in English; contains passages in French and Spanish.

_____ Intended audience: High school civics classes.

_____ Accompanied by second back-up disk; copy-protected.

_____ Summary: Follows the Republican campaign for U.S. president in the 1996 election.

_____ Data collected 1994-1995.

Computer animation

_____ Title on manual: Graphics animation how-to.

_____ System requirements: IBM Pentium or higher; 1 MB RAM; CD player and drive.

_____ File size varies.

_____ Thesis (M.A.) -- Ithaca College, 1998.

_____ User's manual by Crane Laws.

_____ Computer game.

_____ Summary.

_____ Copy-protected.

_____ Title from title screen.

_____ Edition statement from container label.

4.3. Computer Files, Error Identification Exercises

The number of errors in each record is given in parentheses at the top of the record. Find the errors and circle them. Write the corrections above the errors. The errors may be in spelling, tags, indicators, subfields, punctuation, etc.

4.3.1. (14 errors)

101 1	≠a Zaron, E.	
245 40	≠a Super-text form letter module [computer file].	
250	≠v Version 1.0	
260	≠a Baltimore, N.Y. : ≠b Muse Software, ≠c 3 1/2 in.	
538	≠a System requirements: computer, printer.	
504	≠a Title from titel screen.	
520	≠Summary: To be used with form letter file created using the program Super-text file, and address file created using Muse Address book program.	
650 0	≠a Correspondence (Commercial)	
710 2	≠a Muse Sofware, Inc.	
753	≠a Computer.	

4.3.2. (19 errors)

100 01	≠a Conrad, John R.
245 00	≠a Spelling bee games ≠h [machine-readable data file].
260	≠a California : ≠b Edu-Ware Services, ≠c 1981.
300	≠a 4 program files on 1 computer disk ; sd., col. : ≠c 3 1/2 in. + 1 guide.
440 0	≠s DragonWare
538	≠a Game paddles.
500	≠a Manide written by Sandy Blumstrom.
505	≠a Squadron -- Skyhook -- Puzzle -- Convoy.
525	≠a Word and letter play for early spelling and rdng readiness skills.
650 1	≠a English language ≠y Orthograph and spelling.
710 10	≠a Blumstrom (Sandy)
710 2	≠a Edu-Ware Services (Firm)
753	≠a Apple II, Atari

4.3.3. (29 errors)

245 00   ≠a Shotgun wounds to the abdominal :≠h [interactive media] / ≠c produced by HumRRO, Human Resources Research Organization, in conjunction with Media Exchange.

245 10   ≠a The patient in shock.

251   ≠a Verson 2.0

256   ≠a Computer data and program.

260 0   ≠a San Diego, Calif. ; ≠b Intelligent Images ; ≠c c1984.

300   ≠a 1 videodisc : sd., col. with b&w ; ≠s 12 cm.

301   ≠a 1 computer disk ; ≠c 5 1/4 in.

302   ≠a 1 guide.

490 0   ≠a Dxter. Emergency/critical care ; ≠p 1010061

500   ≠a Videodisc: Pioneer or Sony videodisc player.

500   ≠a Computer disk: IBM XT or higher; 640K; IBM InfoWindow system or compatible.

500   ≠a Title from videodisc lable.

501   ≠a Variant title on guide: The the patient in shock.

502   "CD-ROM contains text data base and floppy disc contains the installation/retrieval software"--package.

511   ≠a Credits: David Allan, Gail Walaven; William C. Shoemaker.

650 0   ≠a Gunshot wounds.

4.3.4. (16 errors)

245 00   ≠t Interactive technology sampler ≠a [videorecording] ≠C from the National Library of Medicine.

256   ≠a Program.

260   ≠a Bethesda, MD. : The National Library, ≠a 1990.

300   ≠a 1 videodisc : ≠b col., sd. ; ≠c 12 in. ≠e 1 leaflet.

538   ≠a System rqmts. : Sony Pioneer models 6000 or 8000 with keypad for Level II or Laser Barcode compatible player with barcode wand.

510   ≠a Subtitle on leaflet: A videodisc of applications in ehalth care.

500   ≠a Issued also as interactive media with separate computer disks for IBM or Macintosh versions.

508   ≠a Producers: Craig Locatis ... [and others].

710 1   ≠a Craig Locatis.

710 1   ≠a National Library of Medicine (U.S.)

4.3.5. (12 errors)

240 10   ≠a Laboratory medicine video library ≠h [videorecording] : ≠b atlas of hematology / ≠c a collaborative effort of the University of Washington departments and facilities and the Health Science Videodisc Development Group.

256   ≠a [Seattle, Wash., D.C.] : ≠b The University, ≠y 1985.

300   ≠a 1 videodisc : ≠b silent, col. ; ≠c 12 in. + 1 guide.

508   ≠a Editor/producer, James Fine ; principal microscopes, Yvonne Betson, Marilyn Ostertag.

650 0   ≠s Pharmacopeia ≠x Computer programs.

700 10   ≠a James, Fine.

4.3.6. (10 errors)

245 14   ≠a The reality of youth ≠h [machine-readable data file] / ≠c conducted by Robert B. Sharp, Inc.

246 14   ≠a 501 survey of youth.

256   ≠a Version 9.155

256   ≠a Computer data (2 files : 1457, 2797 recordings).

261   ≠a Albuquerque, N.M. : ≠b 501 Inc., ≠c 1997.

500   ≠a Title from codebook.

500   ≠a Also called 501 servay of youth.

501   ≠a Documented written by: Rob Sharp and Carol B. Sharp.

538   ≠a Mode of access: Mainframe computer in a time-sharing environment.

650 10   ≠a Sharp, Robert B.

4.3.7. (7 errors)

245 00   ≠a Desert Strom ≠a [Interactive Multimedia] : ≠b the war in the Persian Gulf / ≠c Warner New Media in association with Time Magazine.

260   ≠a Burbank, CA : ≠b Warner New Media, ≠c 1991.

300   ≠a 1 computer optical disc : sd., col. ; 5 in.

548   ≠a System requirements: Macintosh Plus or newer; at least 1M RAM (color machines require 2M RAM); System 6.0.5 or later; Apple-compatible SCSI CD-ROM drive.

500   ≠a Title from title screens.

650 0   ≠a Persian Gulf War, 1991.

4.3.8. (1 error)

245 04 ≠a Big band instruments ≠h [interactive multimedia] : ≠b the instruments are for us.

256 ≠a Computer data and program.

260 ≠a Selina, Kansas : ≠b Sewell Music Co., ≠c c1996.

300 ≠a 1 computer optical disc : ≠b sd. ; ≠c 4 3/4 in. + ≠e 1 instruction booklet.

440 0 ≠a Sewell audio notes

538 ≠a System requirements: Macintosh computer; at least 2M of memory; system software 6.0.5 or later; HyperCard 2.0 or greater; hard disk drive with at least 5M of free space; audio playback equipment; Apple CD SC CD-ROM drive or compatible.

500 ≠a Title from disc label.

500 ≠a Annotated by Jimmie Smith.

500 ≠a Music by Willie Sewell; plays as pure audio on regular CD players.

520 ≠a An interactive multimedia introduction to instruments from the big band era. Includes music, photographs, on-screen commentary and annotation, historical information, sounds, and musical analysis by Mary Helen Smith.

650 0 ≠a Big bands ≠x Software.

700 1 ≠a Smith, Jimmie.

700 1 ≠a Smith, Mary Helen.

700 1 ≠a Sewell, Willie.

4.4. Computer Files, 008 (Header) Information

The codes given here are specifically for computer files. Use them to create 008 fields for the records in the exercises following the code list.

00–05 Date entered on file; indicates the date the record was created; recorded in the pattern *yymmdd* (year/year/month/month/day/day).

06 Type of date/publication status. One-character code that categorizes the type of dates given in 008/07–10 (Date 1) and 008/11–14 (Date 2). For serials, 008/06 also indicates the publication status.

(blank)—No dates given; B.C. date involved. Each character in fields 008/07–10 and 008/11–14 contains a blank (.).

c—Serial item currently published. 008/07–10 contains the beginning date of publication; 008/11–14 contains 9999.

d—Serial item ceased publication. 008/07–10 contains beginning date of publication; 008/11–14 contains ending date.

e—Detailed date; 008/07–10 contains year and 008/11–14 contains month and day, recorded as *mmdd*.

i—Inclusive dates of collection.

    k—Range of years of bulk of collection.

    m—Multiple dates; 008/07–10 usually contains the beginning date and 008/11–14 contains the ending date.

    n—Dates unknown; each position in 008/07–10 and 008/11–14 contains blanks.

    p—Date of distribution/release/issue and production/recording session when different.

    q—Questionable date; 008/07–10 contains the earliest possible date; 008/11–14 contains the latest possible date.

    r—Reprint/reissue date and original date; 008/07–10 contains the date of reproduction or reissue (i.e., the most current date) and 008/11–14 contains the date of the original, if known.

    s—Single known/probable date. 008/07–10 contains the date; 008/11–14 contains blanks.

    t—Publication date and copyright date.

    u—Serial status unknown. 008/07–10 contains the beginning date of publication; 008/11–14 contains 9999.

07–10   (Date 1)

    (blank)—Date element is not applicable.

    u—Date element is totally or partially unknown.

11–14   (Date 2)

    (blank)—Date element is not applicable.

    u—Date element is totally or partially unknown.

15–17   Place of publication, production, or execution. A two- or three-character code that indicates the place of publication, production, or execution. Two-character codes are left-justified and the unused position contains a blank. [Codes for the United States consist of the two-letter ZIP code abbreviation plus *u* for United States. New York, for example, would be coded *nyu*.] Unless otherwise specified, codes are always lower-case letters.

18–21   Undefined. Each contains a blank (.) or a fill character (|).

22   Target audience.

    (blank)—Unknown or not specified

    a—Preschool

    b—Primary

    c—Elementary and junior high school

    d—Secondary (senior high school)

    e—Adult

    f—Specialized

    g—General

    j—Juvenile

23–25　Undefined. Each contains a blank (.) or a fill character (|).

26　　　Type of computer code.

　　　　a—Numeric data

　　　　b—Computer program

　　　　c—Representational (pictorial or graphic information that can be manipulated in conjunction with other types of files to produce graphic patterns that can be used to interpret and give meaning to the information).

　　　　d—Document

　　　　e—Bibliographic data

　　　　f—Font

　　　　g—Game

　　　　h—Sound

　　　　i—Interactive multimedia

　　　　j—Online system or service

　　　　m—Combination

　　　　u—Unknown

　　　　z—Other

27　　　Undefined. Each contains a blank (.) or a fill character (|).

28　　　Government publication. A one-character code indicating whether the item is published or produced by or for a government agency, and if so, the jurisdictional level of the agency.

　　　　(blank)—Not a government publication

　　　　a—Autonomous or semi-autonomous component

　　　　c—Multilocal

　　　　f—Federal/national

　　　　i—International/intergovernmental

　　　　l—Local

　　　　m—Multistate

　　　　o—Government publication—level undetermined

　　　　s—State, provincial, territorial, dependent, etc.

　　　　u—Unknown if item is government publication or not

　　　　z—Other

29–34　Undefined. Each contains a blank (.) or fill character (|).

35–37　Language. A three-character code indicating the language of the item.

38　　　Modified record. A one-character code that indicates whether any data in a bibliographic record is a modification of information that appeared on the item being cataloged or that was intended to be included in the USMARC record. Codes are assigned a priority, and, when more than one code applies to the item, are recorded in the order of the following list.

(blank)—Not modified.

d—Dashed-on information.

o—Completely romanized/printed in script.

s—Shortened. Some data omitted because the record would have exceeded the maximum length allowed by a particular system.

x—Missing characters. Characters could not be converted into machine-readable form due to character set limitations.

39   Cataloging source. A one-character code that indicates the creator of the original cataloging record. The NUC symbol or the name of the organization may be contained in subfield ≠a of field 040.

(blank)—Library of Congress

a—National Agricultural Library

b—National Library of Medicine

c—Library of Congress cooperative cataloging program

d—Other sources [most libraries fall here]

n—Report to *New Serial Titles*

u—Unknown

Computer Files, 008 (Header) Information Exercises

4.4.1.   Target audience

a. _____ First grade

b. _____ Primary

c. _____ Secondary school

d. _____ Adult

e. _____ General

4.4.2.   Type of computer file

a. _____ Interactive multimedia

b. _____ Game

c. _____ Numeric data

d. _____ Document

e. _____ Font

f. _____ Online system or service

g. _____ Other

h. _____ Computer program

4.4.3.   Government publication

    a. ____ Multilocal

    b. ____ State, provincial, territorial, dependent, etc.

    c. ____ Federal

    d. ____ Multistate

    e. ____ Autonomous or semi-autonomous component

    f. ____ Local

    g. ____ Not a government publication

Fill in the 008 field with the correct codes.

4.4.4.   008   . . . .

    100 1   ≠a Stinson, Douglas B.

    240 3   ≠a Write away.

    245 10   ≠a Midwest Software Associates present Write away ≠h [computer file] : ≠b a word processing/communications system / ≠c by Douglas B. Stinson.

    246 30   ≠a Write away.

    260   ≠a St. Louis, MO : ≠b Midwest Software Associates, ≠c c1984.

    300   ≠a 1 computer disk ; ≠c 3 1/2 in. + ≠e manual and command card.

    538   ≠a System requirements: Apple II; 80 column card; modem; printer.

4.4.5.   008   . . . .

    100 1   ≠a Ashwell, Jonathan D.

    245 10   ≠a Bookends ≠h [computer file] /≠c by Jonathan D. Ashwell.

    260   ≠a West Bloomfield, Mich. : ≠b Sensible Software, ≠c c1983.

    300   ≠a 6 program files on 1 computer disk ; ≠c 5 1/4 in. + ≠e 1 manual (93 p.)

    538   ≠a System requirements: Apple II, II+, IIe, III ; 48K; 40-column display device.

    520   ≠a Program for saving, indexing and formatting references for books, magazines, journals, etc., and for formatting bibliographies.

4.4.6.   008   . . . .

    100 1   ≠a Ashwell, Jonathan D.

    245 10   ≠a Bookends extended ≠h [computer file] : ≠b the reference management system / ≠c Jonathan D. Ashwell.

    250   ≠a Version 2.11

    260   ≠a Birmingham, Mich. : ≠b Sensible Software, ≠c 1985.

300	≠a 6 program files on 1 computer disk ; ≠c 5 1.4 in. + ≠e 1 compact disc (3 1/2 in.) and 1 manual.
538	≠a System requirements: Apple IIe (with Apple Extended 80-column text card) or Apple IIC; 128K. Optional items: printer (up to 136 columns strongly recommended), additional disk drives and/or hard disk drive.
520	≠a Program for indexing books, magazines, and journals, and for formatting bibliographies.

4.4.7.   008   . . . .

245 00	≠a Electronic world atlas ≠h [computer file].
250	≠a IBM version.
256	≠a Graphics (maps and photographs)
260	≠a Baton Rouge, La. : ≠b Ferguson Frolics, ≠c c1993.
300	≠a 1 computer disk : ≠b col. ; ≠c 3 1/2 in.
500	≠a Title from title screen.
500	≠a Accompanied by documentation (67 p. : ill. ; 22 cm.)
538	≠a System requirements: 486 or higher; minimum 4MB (8 MB recommended); Windows 95.

4.4.8.   008   . . . .

245 00	≠a Alien attacker! ≠h [computer file].
250	≠a Version 2.01.
256	≠a Computer data and program
260	≠a Baton Rouge, La. : ≠b Ferguson Frolics, ≠c c1994.
300	≠a 1 computer optical disc : ≠b sd., col. ; ≠c 4 3/4 in.
516	≠a Program (Retrieval software); Graphics.
538	≠a Game card; joystick; sound card; VGA graphics recommended.

4.4.9.   008   . . . .

245 00	≠a Natural hazard protection and prevention ≠h [computer file].
246 10	≠a Hurricanes, tornadoes, and other natural hazards.
256	≠a Computer data and programs
260	≠a New Orleans, La. : ≠b Hurricane Research Center, ≠c c1989-
538	≠a Mode of access: Internet. Host: hrc.uno.edu. Available at URL: http://hrc.uno.edu/
500	≠a Title from title screen.
500	≠a HRC home page created Nov. 1994 by Sandra McIntyre-Colby.
856 7	≠2 http ≠z http://hrc.uno.edu/

4.4.10. 008 . . . .

245 00 ≠a Native American program, Louisiana State University at Eunice ≠h [computer file].

256 ≠a Computer data

260 ≠a Baton Rouge : ≠b Native American program, LSU at Eunice, ≠c [1991-]

538 1 ≠a Mode of access: Internet. Host: lsue.edu. Available at URL: http://lsue.edu/nap/

500 ≠a Title from title screen.

500 ≠a Site maintained by Ajaye Bloomstone.

520 ≠a Develops, evaluates, and compiles data on native Americans living in southwest Louisiana. Documents changes over the years and maintains records and historical documents.

4.4.11. 008 . . . .

245 00 ≠a Autocat ≠h [computer file] : ≠b library cataloging and authorities discussion group.

246 10 ≠a Library cataloging and authorities discussion group.

256 ≠a Computer data

260 ≠a [Buffalo, N.Y. : ≠b State University of New York at Buffalo, host], ≠c 1990-

538 ≠a Mode of access: Internet e-mail; host: ubvm.cc.buffalo.edu. Subscribe via e-mail message to: (Internet) listserv@ubvm.cc.buffalo.edu or (Bitnet) listserv@ubvm, with message: subscribe autocat [firstname lastname].

538 ≠a Also available as a Usenet newsgroup: bit.listserv.autocat.

500 ≠a Title from header file.

500 ≠a Founded Oct. 1990 by Nancy Keane at the University of Vermont; transferred Apr. 26, 1993 to the University at Buffalo.

856 ≠a ubvm.cc.buffalo.edu ≠a Autocat ≠h Listserv ≠i subscribe ≠m Judith Hopkins (ulcjh@ubvm.cc.buffalo.edu) ≠m Douglas Winship (winship@tenet.edu) ≠n State University of New York at Buffalo, Buffalo, N.Y.

4.5. Computer Files, *AACR2R* Chapter 9 Exercises

4.5.1.   What do the rules in *AACR2R* Chapter 9 cover?

4.5.2.   What do the rules in Chapter 9 *not* cover?

4.5.3.   When would you record a file name or a data set name as the title proper?

4.5.4.   What type of information might be recorded in the edition area for computer files?

4.5.5.   If an edition statement appears in the documentation, but does not specify if the statement applies to the documentation or the software, do you record it in the software bibliographic record?

4.5.6.   What specific material designations (SMDs) are used with computer files?

4.5.7.   If the item being cataloged is not one of the SMDs in question 4.5.6, what do you do?

4.5.8.   Where do you find instructions for giving details of accompanying material?

4.5.9.   What is the chief source of information for computer files?

4.5.10.   If the agency cataloging the computer file has no equipment to read the computer file, where should cataloging data come from?

4.5.11.   What general material designation (GMD) do you use if there are materials falling into two or more categories?

4.5.12.   If the source of the edition of a computer file is different from the source of the title proper, how do you denote the difference?

4.5.13.   What terms do you use to indicate the type of computer file?

4.5.14.   When do you indicate that a computer file has sound?

4.5.15.   Which note should be given first on a bibliographic record? How do you know?

4.5.16.   How should you catalog a work of several separate items, usually a work of interactive multimedia, if the title information varies on the different pieces?

4.5.17.   Must you always include a general material designation when cataloging computer file materials?

4.5.18.   What words alert you to suspect that the item you're cataloging is a different edition?

4.5.19.   What information do you give in the 256 field?

4.5.20.   If the information on file characteristics is not readily available, what do you do?

4.5.21.   How do you record the dimensions of computer disks and cartridges?

4.5.22.   What is the order of notes as given in *AACR2R*?

4.5.23.   If you take the title from the title screen(s) of the item, do you have to give the source of the title proper in a note?

4.5.24.   Who is listed in the 245 field in the statement of responsibility?

4.5.25.   When the item being cataloged has minor changes such as corrections of misspellings, changes in the arrangement of the contents, or changes in the display medium or physical characteristics, do you enter the item as a new edition?

4.5.26.   How do you record publishing information from an unpublished item?

4.5.27.   Which type of computer carrier does not require details of dimension?

4.5.28.   Are terms of availability ever qualified?

5.

MAPS

Maps have been around for thousands of years, and continue to be extremely helpful. There are maps of campuses, library buildings, cities, states, countries, and the world. Maps take the form of wall hangings, postcards, placemats, jigsaw puzzles, and globes. The most widely used maps are road maps and graphic representations. There are maps of the stars, oceans, planets, and even imaginary places. Cataloging maps can be a lot of fun.

There are many notes in map bibliographic records. Notes deal with the intellectual content of the map, or its boundaries, inset or ancillary maps, parallel titles and other title information, orientation to a direction other than north, and more.

Maps may be printed on paper, vellum, linen, or plastic; they may be cartographically or pictorially drawn; they may show relief by hachures, spot heights, isolines, or contours.

Determining the scale of a map may be a problem, as scale must be expressed as a representative fraction. The publisher of the map may give the scale in words (1 inch to 4 miles or 5 inches to 3 miles) and the cataloger must convert it to a representative fraction. Sometimes on old maps the scale is not given in inches, feet, or miles, but in arpents or furlongs. Projection types are also confusing to persons not familiar with maps.

Although map cataloging handles more unusual items of information than other nonprint formats, it becomes easier with experience.

5.1. Maps, Full Records Tagging Exercises

Add the proper tags, indicators, and subfields to the bibliographic records given here. The blanks indicate where tags, indicators, and subfields should be placed. Precede each subfield code with a delimiter. You will need to use the USMARC bibliographic formats, *AACR2R*, *LCSH*, and other tools.

5.1.1. 110 _   ____ Louisiana. ____ Dept. of Transportation and Development. ____ Traffic and Planning Division.

        245 _ _   ____ Map of Louisiana showing state-maintained highway system ____ [map].

        246 _ _   ____ Louisiana highway system.

        255   ____ Scales vary.

        260   ____ [Baton Rouge] : ____ The Division, ____ 1992.

        300   ____ 92 maps : ____ b&w ; ____ 44 × 49 cm. on sheets 47 × 63 cm.

        500   ____ Some maps include index and/or location insert.

        500   ____ Also includes 1992 Louisiana railway system, official control section maps for districts, and detailed maps of each parish.

5.1.2. 110 _ _   ____ Committee for the Preservation of the Port Hudson Battlefield.

        245 _ _   ____ A collection of maps for those persons interested in Port Hudson Battlefield ____ [map].

        246 _ _   ____ Port Hudson Battlefield.

        255   ____ Scales vary.

        260   ____ [Baton Rouge, La.] : ____ The Committee, ____ c1964.

        300   ____ 14 maps : ____ some col. ; ____ 58 × 45 cm. – 72 × 90 cm. + ____ 1 text (5 leaves).

        500   ____ Title from cover of portfolio.

5.1.3. 1__ _   ____ Louisiana. ____ Dept. of Public Works.

        2__ _ _   ____ [Old levee drawings concerning Port Allen and W.B.R. Parish] ____ [map].

        2__ _ _   ____ Port Allen levees.

        2__ _ _   ____ West Baton Rouge Parish levees.

        2__   ____ Scales vary.

        2__   ____ [Port Allen, La.] : ____ R.D. Landry, ____ 1976.

        3__   ____ 10 maps : ____ b&w ; ____ 40 × 50 cm. on sheets 45 × 64 cm. + ____ 2 sheets of explanatory notes.

        5__   ____ Title supplied by cataloger taken from attached in-house label.

        5__   ____ Photoprint from microfilm.

5.1.4.　1__ _　____ West Baton Rouge Parish (La.). ____ Assessor's Office.

　　　　2__ _ _　____ West Baton Rouge Parish ____ [map] : ____ index to rural maps.

　　　　2__ _ _　____ Index to rural maps.

　　　　2__　____ Scales vary.

　　　　2__　____ [Port Allen, La. : ____ The Office, ____ 198-?]

　　　　3__　____ 1 map : ____ photocopy ; ____ 73 × 96 cm. on sheet 76 × 106 cm.

　　　　5__　____ Blue line print.

　　　　5__　____ With enlargements of Wards 2, 3, and 4.

5.1.5.　1__ _　____ Ashburn Maps.

　　　　2__ _ _　____ City map of Alexandria and Pineville ____ [map] / ____ Ashburn Maps ; compliments of Stephens Agency, Inc.

　　　　2__　____ Scale [ca. 1:23344] ; ____ 1:380160.

　　　　2__　____ Fort Worth, Tex. : ____ Ashburn Maps, ____ 1971.

　　　　3__　____ 1 map : ____ col. ; ____ 58 × 43 cm., folded to 23 × 11 cm.

　　　　5__　____ Scale is given as 1 1/4 inch to 1/2 mile.

　　　　5__　____ Includes street indexes.

　　　　5__　____ Panel title.

　　　　5__　____ Includes inset map of England Air Force Base.

　　　　5__　____ Includes ancillary maps of Rapides Parish, Pineville Central Business District and Alexandria Central Business District.

　　　　6__ _　____ Alexandria (La.) ____ Maps.

　　　　6__ _　____ Pineville (La.) ____ Maps.

　　　　6__ _　____ Rapides Parish (La.) ____ Maps.

5.1.6.　1__ _　____ Crawford, Andrew, ____ Surveyor.

　　　　2__ _ _　____ Plan of the United States public grounds, Baton Rouge, La. ____ [map] / ____ A. Crawford, surveyor.

　　　　2__　____ Scale 1:4800.

　　　　2__　____ [S.l. : ____ s.n.], ____ 1839.

　　　　3__　____ 1 map ; ____ 45 × 61 cm.

　　　　5__　____ References list the number of acres of swamp, woodland, etc., and the number of acres in lots such as hospital lot and ordnance lot.

　　　　5__　____ Magnetic variation 8°45' E. on recto.

　　　　5__　____ Selected buildings and trees shown pictorially.

　　　　5__　____ "C-109-2"

　　　　6__ _　____ Baton Rouge (La.) ____ Maps.

5.1.7. ___ _   ____ United States. ____ Commodity Stabilization Service.

___ __ _   ____ E. Baton Rouge Parish, Louisiana ____ [map] / ____ U.S. Department of Agriculture, Commodity Stabilization Service.

___   ____ Scale 1:20,000.

___   ____ [Washington, D.C.] : ____ The Service, ____ 1959.

___   ____ 1 remote-sensing image ; ____ 47 × 45 cm.

___   ____ Imaging produced by Coloramic Aerial Surveys Corp., subcontractor, Woltz Studios, Inc., Des Moines, IA.

___ _   ____ East Baton Rouge Parish (La.) ____ Maps.

___ _   ____ Aerial photographs.

___ _   ____ Coloramic Aerial Surveys Corp.

___ _   ____ Woltz Studios.

This one is all yours—no help, no tips, no blanks. Good luck.

5.1.8.   ___ _ _   Plan of Fort Baton Rouge [map].

___   Scale [ca. 1:6,480].

___   [S.l. : s.n., 1800?]

___   1 map : photocopy ; 31 × 54 cm.

___   In: Collot, Georges Henri Victor. A journey in North America ... 1924. pl. #35.

___   Oriented with north to the left.

___   Scale is given in fathoms; 1 fathom equals 6 feet.

___   Fort, selected buildings and trees shown pictorially.

___   Relief shown by shading.

___ _   Fort Baton Rouge (La.) Maps.

___ _   Baton Rouge (La.) Maps.

5.2. Maps, Notes Exercise

Read section 3.7 in *Anglo-American Cataloguing Rules*, 2nd edition, 1988 revision. Use the order given there to put the notes in the bibliographic record here in the correct order. Number the notes from 1 to 10 on the blanks. The projected title is given in bold letters at the top of the exercise.

Plan of the lots reserved for Spanish families of Galvez Town

____ Also issued on microfiche.

____ Library's copy annotated in red ink with family names.

_____ Scale is given using three different measurement terms: percha (Fr.)=16.5 ft., toise (Fr.)=6 ft., and vara (Sp.)=33 in.

_____ Title in English and Spanish.

_____ Accompanied by a translation of the survey information shown on recto.

_____ First published in 1805.

_____ Photocopy.

_____ Title on verso: Lots reserved for Spanish families.

_____ Relief shown by hachures.

_____ Taken from the original series of maps showing land usage for Louisiana Spanish land grants.

5.3. Maps, Error Identification Exercises

The number of errors in each record is given in parentheses at the top of the record. Find the errors and circle them. Write the corrections above the errors. The errors may be in spelling, tags, indicators, subfields, punctuation, etc.

5.3.1. (10 errors)

100 1   ≠a Miller, Smith, & Champagne, inc.

245 20   ≠a West Baton Rouge Parish roads [map].

255   ≠a 1:63,360.

260 0   ≠a [Baton Rouge, La.] : ≠B Miller, Champagne, and Smith, ≠c 1992.

300   ≠a 1 map : ≠b photocopy ; ≠c 71 × 51 cm. ≠c on sheet 107 × 77 cm.

505   ≠a Blue line print.

500   ≠a Includes location insets.

650 0   ≠a West Baton Rouge Parish (La.) ≠x Road maps.

5.3.2. (17 errors)

110 1   ≠a Albert, Gerald, ≠c 1917-

245 14   ≠a Road closings in Richmond County, October 1977 ≠h [maps].

255 2   ≠a Scale: 1-63300.

301   ≠a 1 map ; ≠b col. ; ≠a 28 cm.

440 4   ≠a Road closures, Richmond County

500   ≠a Orinted with north to top left.

504   ≠a Intended tobe given out to the public.

651 0   ≠a Richmond County, Virginia ≠z Road maps.

5.3.3. (25 errors)

100 2   ≠a Geological Survey (U.S.A.)

245 14   ≠a Miami quadrangle, Florida--Dade Co., 1988 ≠h (map) : ≠b 7.5 minute series (topogrphic) / ≠c mapped, edited and published by the Geological Survey.

255 2   ≠a Scale 1-24,000 ; ≠b transverse Mercator proj. ≠c (w80°15'00" ; w80°07'30" by n25°52'30" ; n25°45'00").

260   ≠b Reston, Virginia : ≠b The Survey ; ≠a Denver, Colorado : For sale by the Survey, ≠c [1992] .

301   ≠a 1 map ; ≠b col. ; ≠a 28 cm.

504 4   ≠a Relief shown by contours, spot heights, and contours.

500   ≠a Deaths shown by isolines and soundings.

504   ≠a "Map photoinspected 1990; no major culture or drainage observed."--Map verso.

500   Includes quadrangle location map.

500   ≠a "DMA 4935 I SW ; ≠v Series V847"

651 0   ≠a Florida ≠z Maps, topographic.

5.3.4. (13 errors)

220 2   ≠a Satellite Snaps, Inc.

245 00   ≠a Fort Lauderdale from LANDSAT 5 / ≠c this print produced and distributed

by Satellite Snaps, Inc. ; image enhancement by KRS Remote Sensing ; Landsat

data distributed by the Earth Observation Satellite Company.

256   ≠a Scale not given.

260   ≠a [Ridgely, Maryland : ≠b Satellite Snaps, ≠c c1999.

300   ≠a 1 remote sensing image : ≠b sd., col. ; ≠c 90 × 46 cm.

300   ≠a Landsat remote sensing image, processed to simulate natural color.

500   Shows Fort Lauderdale metropolitan area.

589   ≠a Library's copy encapsulated in plastic.

650 0   ≠a Remote sensing ≠z Fort Lauderdale Region, Florida.

650 0   ≠a Fort Lauderdale Region (Fla.) ≠x Photographic maps.

5.3.5. (18 errors)

110   ≠a Morocco. ≠B Idarat al-Maadin wa-al-Jiyulujiyah.

245 10   ≠a Carte tectonique internationale de l'Afrique. ≠b International tectonic map

of Africa. ≠c compiled by the Geological Survey of Morocco.

260   ≠a [Paris] : ≠b Association of African Geological Surveys, ≠c c1969.

301   ≠a col. map ; ≠c 182 × 182 cm. on 9 sheets 68 × 98 - 68 × 93 centimeters.

440 0   ≠a Earth sciences ; ≠v4

507   ≠a Scale 1:5,000,000

600   ≠a Depths shown by contours and soundings.

504   ≠a Includes indx map and inset.

500   ≠a Shows tectonics information as of 1694.

651 0   ≠a Geology ≠x Africa ≠z Maps.

5.3.6. (10 errors)

110 20   ≠a Kneeland, Ira C.

240 11   ≠a [Baton Rouge] ≠h [map] / ≠c Ira C. Kneeland, surveyor.

255   Scale not given.

260   ≠a [S.l.] : ≠b [s.n.] ; ≠c 1809.

300   ≠a 1 map : ≠b Xerox copy : ≠c 54 × 38 cm.

500   ≠a Title supplied by cataloger.

500   ≠y "1809" handwritten in lower left hand corner.

560   ≠a Shows four public lots for the use of the church, etc.

655 7   ≠a Baton Rouge (La.) ≠x Maps.

5.3.7. (1 error)

110 1   ≠a United States. ≠b National Ocean Service.

246 10   ≠a Miami to Marathon and Florida Bay, Florida ≠h [map] / ≠c National

Ocean Service.

255   ≠a Scale 1:80,000 : ≠b Mercator proj.

260   ≠a Washington D.C. : ≠b The Service, ≠c 1992.

300   ≠a 1 map on 4 sheets : ≠b both sides, col. ; ≠c sheets 37 × 83 cm., folded to

37 × 23 cm., in folder 38 × 23 cm.

490 1   ≠a Nautical chart ; ≠v 11451

500   ≠a Depths shown by isolines and soundings.

500   ≠a Includes 7 illustrations and nautical chart diagram.

500   ≠a Folder includes tide information chart and facilities chart.

650   0   ≠a Intracoastal waterways ≠z Florida ≠x Maps.

810 1   ≠a United States. ≠b National Ocean Service. ≠t Nautical chart ; ≠v 11451.

5.3.8. (23 errors)

120 1   ≠a Great Britain. ≠b Ordinance Survey.

245 14   ≠a Caman Islands, visitors map ≠h [map] / ≠c nade and published by the

           Ordnance Survay, Southampton, England, with the asstance of the Cayman

           Islands Government.

255   ≠a Scale 1:50,000 ≠a (W 81°25'--W 79°45'/N 19°45'--N19°15').

260   ≠x Southhampton : ≠b The Survay ; ≠a Grand Caman, Cayman Islands : ≠b

           Dept. of Tourism, ≠c 1989.

300   ≠a 3 maps on 1 sheet : ≠b col. ; ≠a 36 × 76 in. or smaller, sheet 79 by 99 in.,

           folded to 20 × 13 in.

504   ≠a Panel titel.

520   ≠a Includes text, location map, and ancillary maps of "Air communications"

           and "George Town."

505 3   ≠a Grand Cayman -- Little Caman -- Caiman Brac.

651   0   ≠a Caiman Islands ≠x Tourist maps.

5.4. Maps, 008 (Header) Information

The codes given here are specifically for maps. Use them to create 008 fields for the records in the exercises following the codes.

00–05   Date entered on file; indicates the date the record was created; recorded in the pattern *yymmdd* (year/year/month/month/day/day).

06   Type of date/publication status. One-character code that categorizes the type of dates given in 008/07–10 (Date 1) and 008/11–14 (Date 2). For serials, 008/06 also indicates the publication status.

> (blank)—No dates given; B.C. date involved. Each character in fields 008/07–10 and 008/11–14 contains a blank (.).

> c—Serial item currently published. 008/07–10 contains the beginning date of publication; 008/11–14 contains 9999.

> d—Serial item ceased publication. 008/07–10 contains beginning date of publication; 008/11–14 contains ending date.

> e—Detailed date; 008/07–10 contains year and 008/11–14 contains month and day, recorded as *mmdd*.

> i—Inclusive dates of collection.

> k—Range of years of bulk of collection.

> m—Multiple dates; 008/07–10 usually contains the beginning date and 008/11–14 contains the ending date.

> n—Dates unknown; each position in 008/07–10 and 008/11–14 contains blanks.

> p—Date of distribution/release/issue and production/recording session when different.

> q—Questionable date; 008/07–10 contains the earliest possible date; 008/11–14 contains the latest possible date.

> r—Reprint/reissue date and original date; 008/07–10 contains the date of reproduction or reissue (i.e., the most current date) and 008/11–14 contains the date of the original, if known.

> s—Single known/probable date. 008/07–10 contains the date; 008/11–14 contains blanks.

> t—Publication date and copyright date.

> u—Serial status unknown. 008/07–10 contains the beginning date of publication; 008/11–14 contains 9999.

07–10   (Date 1)

> (blank)—Date element is not applicable.

> u—Date element is totally or partially unknown.

11–14   (Date 2)

(blank)—Date element is not applicable.

u—Date element is totally or partially unknown.

15–17   Place of publication, production, or execution. A two- or three-character code that indicates the place of publication, production, or execution. Two-character codes are left-justified and the unused position contains a blank. [Codes for the United States consist of the two-letter ZIP code abbreviation plus *u* for United States. New York, for example, would be coded *nyu*.] Unless otherwise specified, codes are always lower-case letters.

18–21   Relief. Up to four one-character codes that indicate the relief type specified on the item. Codes are recorded in order of their importance to the described item. If fewer than four codes are assigned, the codes are left-justified and each unused position contains a blank.

(blank)—No relief shown

a—Contours

b—Shading

c—Gradient tints

d—Hachures

e—Bathymetry/soundings

f—Form lines

g—Spot heights

i—Pictorially

j—Land forms

k—Bathymetry/isolines

z—Other relief type

22–23   Projection

(blank)—Projection not specified

aa—Aitoff

ab—Gnomic

ac—Lambert's azimuthal equal area

ad—Orthographic

ae—Azimuthal equidistant

af—Stereographic

ag—General vertical near-sided

am—Modified stereographic for Alaska

ap—Polar stereographic

au—Azimuthal, specific type unknown

ba—Gall

bb—Goode's homolographic

bc—Lambert's cylindrical equal area

bd—Mercator

be—Miller

bf—Mollweide

bg—Sinusoidal

bh—Transverse Mercator

bj—Equirectangular

bo—Oblique Mercator

br—Robinson

bs—Space oblique Mercator

bu—Cylindrical, specific type unknown

ca—Alber's equal area

cb—Bonne

cc—Lambert's conformal conic

ce—Equidistant conic

cp—Polyconic

cu—Conic, specific type unknown

da—Armadillo

db—Butterfly

dc—Eckert

dd—Goode's homolosine

de—Miller's bipolar oblique conformal conic

df—Van Der Grinten

dg—Dimaxion

dh—Cordiform

zz—Other

24   Prime meridian. A one-character code that indicates the named longitude from which east and west are calculated on the item.

(blank)—Prime meridian not specified

e—Greenwich

f—Fero

g—Paris

p—Philadelphia

w—Washington, D.C.

z—Other

25   Type of cartographic material

a—Single map

b—Map series

c—Map serial

d—Globe

e—Atlas

26–27   Undefined. Each contains a blank (.) or a fill character (|).

28   Government publication. A one-character code indicating whether the item is published or produced by or for a government agency, and if so, the jurisdictional level of the agency.

(blank)—Not a government publication

a—Autonomous or semi-autonomous component

c—Multilocal

f—Federal/national

i—International/intergovernmental

l—Local

m—Multistate

o—Government publication—level undetermined

s—State, provincial, territorial, dependent, etc.

u—Unknown if item is government publication or not

z—Other

29-30   Undefined. Each contains a blank (.) or fill character (|).

31   Index

0—No index

1—Index is present

32   Undefined. Each contains a blank (.) or a fill character (|).

33–34   Special format characteristics

(blank)—No specified special format characteristics

e—Manuscript

j—Picture card, post card

k—Calendar

l—Puzzle

m—Braille

n—Game

o—Wall map

p—Playing cards

q—Large print

r—Loose-leaf

z—Other

35–37   Language. A three-character code indicating the language of the item.

38   Modified record. A one-character code that indicates whether any data in a bibliographic record is a modification of information that appeared on the item being cataloged or that was intended to be included in the USMARC record. Codes are assigned a priority, and, when more than one code applies to the item, are recorded in the order of the following list.

    (blank)—Not modified.

d—Dashed-on information.

o—Completely romanized/printed in script.

s—Shortened. Some data omitted because the record would have exceeded the maximum length allowed by a particular system.

x—Missing characters. Characters could not be converted into machine-readable form due to character set limitations.

39   Cataloging source. A one-character code that indicates the creator of the original cataloging record. The NUC symbol or the name of the organization may be contained in subfield ≠a of field 040.

    (blank)—Library of Congress

a—National Agricultural Library

b—National Library of Medicine

c—Library of Congress cooperative cataloging program

d—Other sources [most libraries fall here]

n—Report to *New Serial Titles*

u—Unknown

Maps, 008 (Header) Information Exercises

5.4.1.   Relief information

a ____ Bathymetry/isolines

b. ____ Bathymetry/soundings

c. ____ Spot heights

d. ____ Contours

e. ____ Hachures

f. ____ Gradient tints

g. ____ None

h. ____ Other

5.4.2.   Projection

a. ____ Mercator

b. ____ Miller

c. ____ Azimuthal equidistant

d. ____ General vertical near-sided

e. ____ Equirectangular

f. ____ Armadillo

g. ____ Butterfly

h. ____ Space oblique Mercator

i. ____ Dimaxion

j. ____ Bonne

k. ____ Other

5.4.3.   Type of cartographic matter

a. ____ Globe

b. ____ Map series

c. ____ Atlas

d. ____ Single map

e. ____ Map serial

5.4.4.   Government publications

a. ____ Local

b. ____ Federal

c. ____ State

d. ____ International

e. ____ Not governmental

f. ____ Multilocal

g. ____ Multistate

5.4.5.   Special format characteristics

a. ____ Wall map

b. ____ Calendar

c. ____ Puzzle

d. ____ Braille

e. ____ Picture card

f. ____ Large print

g. ____ Loose-leaf

h. ____ Manuscript

Fill in the 008 field with the correct codes.

5.4.6.   008   . . . .

100 1   ≠a Blaeu, Willem Janszoon, ≠d 1571-1638.

245 10   ≠a Americae nova tabula ≠h [map] / ≠c Auct: Guiljelmo Blaeuw.

255   ≠a Scale indeterminable.

260   ≠a New York : ≠b Penn Prints, ≠c [1960].

300   ≠a 1 map : ≠b col. ; ≠c 36 x 46 cm. on sheet 42 x 56 cm.

500   ≠a Relief shown pictorially.

500   ≠a Ten vignettes on sides and nine plans of cities on top.

500   ≠a Shows drainage, settlements, etc.

500   ≠a "Cum privilegio decem Annorum."

500   ≠a Added title: 17th century map of North and South America, by Willem Blaeu.

500   ≠a Publisher's catalog lists map date as 1636.

5.4.7.   008   . . . .

245 00   ≠a Map of the Parish of Avoyelles and part of Rapides Louisiana from United States surveys ≠h [map].

255   ≠a Scale: 1:70,000.

260   ≠a [Washington : Division of Maps, Library of Congress, ≠c 1931].

300   ≠a 1 map on 4 sheets ; ≠c 114 x 75 cm. on sheets 62 x 46 cm.

500   ≠a Includes listing of lands for sale.

500   ≠a "Division of Maps, May 4, 1931, Library of Congress" stamped in lower right hand corner of sheet no. 3.

500   ≠a Reprint. Originally published: New Orleans : McCerran, Landry, & Powell, 1860.

5.4.8.   008   . . . .

100 1   ≠a Robertson, S. B.

245 10   ≠a Map of Avoyelles ph [i.e., Parish], LA ≠h [map] / ≠c compiled from the official surveys by S.B. Robertson, 1879.

255   ≠a Scale 1:52,466.

260   ≠a [Washington : ≠b Map Division, Library of Congress, ≠c 1879]

300   ≠a 1 map on 4 sheets ; ≠c 88 x 86 cm. on sheets 51 x 45 cm.

440 0   ≠a [Land ownership maps] ; ≠v 245

500   ≠a "Map Division, Jan. 30, 1926, Library of Congress" stamped in lower right hand corner of sheet no. 3.

500   ≠a Reprint. Originally published: 1879.

500   ≠a Filed by United States as "Exhibits: Odon Deucatte vs. United States, no. 101."

5.4.9.   008   . . . .

110 2   ≠a Sanborn Map Company.

245 10   ≠a Addis, West Baton Rouge Parish, Louisiana ≠h [map] /
≠c surveyed by Louisiana Fire Prevention Bureau.

255   ≠a Scale 1:600.

260   ≠a New York : ≠b Sanborn, ≠c 1921.

300   ≠a 1 map : ≠b col. ; ≠c 65 × 54 cm.

500   ≠a "October 1920"--recto.

500   ≠a Includes inset maps.

5.4.10.   008   . . . .

245 00   ≠a [Map of land owners on east and west banks of the Mississippi
River of Baton Rouge, La.] ≠h [map].

260   ≠a [S.l. : ≠b s.n., ≠c 1799].

300   ≠a 1 map : ≠b photocopy ; ≠c 30 × 23 cm., on sheet 36 × 28 cm.

500   ≠a Title supplied by cataloger.

500   ≠a "1799" written in upper right hand corner.

500   ≠a In: Arthur, Stanley Clisby. "Old map reveals holdings of residents
here in 1799..." State Times, 4/27/40, p. 1-B : State Times 12/15/42,
p. 18.

5.4.11.   008   . . . .

245 00   ≠a Abbeville 1938 ≠h [map]

255   ≠a Scale 1:4,800.

260   ≠c [1938].

300   ≠a 1 map : ≠b coated textile ; ≠c 20 × 39 cm.

500   ≠a "W.P.A." stamped in lower right corner.

500   ≠a Oriented with north to the right.

5.4.12.   008   . . . .

245 00   ≠a Donaldsonville ≠h [map] : ≠b the fertilizer industry.

255   ≠a Scale indeterminable.

260   ≠a Baton Rouge, La. : ≠b Homesite Co., ≠c c1990.

300   ≠a 1 map : ≠b col. ; ≠c 23 × 22 cm. on sheet 46 × 61 cm.

440 0   ≠a Louisiana petrochemical industry map ; ≠v sec. IV

500   ≠a Each map in series describes a different trend, from general
industry trends to chlorine industry, chemical pipelines, and more.

500   ≠a Aerial photography.

500   ≠a Ancillary map of Louisiana showing location of this item.

500   ≠a Fertilizer companies, addresses and general description flow
charts on recto.

500   ≠a Includes explanation about fertilizers on recto.

5.4.13.   008   . . . .

245 00   ≠a Pierre Part ≠h [map] : ≠b the fishing capital of Louisiana.

255   ≠a Scale indeterminable.

260   ≠a Baton Rouge, La. : ≠b Bass Anglers of BR, ≠c c1992.

300   ≠a 1 map : ≠b col. ; ≠c 23 × 22 cm. on sheet 46 × 61 cm.

440   0   ≠a Louisiana recreational sites map ; ≠v pt. V

500   ≠a Each map in series describes a different type of recreational activity and the best spots for utilizing the resources.

500   ≠a Shows various fishing locations by symbol.

500   ≠a Ancillary map of Louisiana showing location of this item.

500   ≠a Includes identification information for various species.

5.5. Maps, *AACR2R* Chapter 3 Exercises

5.5.1.   What types of materials does "cartographic materials" include, according to *AACR2R*?

5.5.2.   What types of materials does "cartographic materials" *not* include?

5.5.3.   When an item has no title, how do you indicate the place it shows?

5.5.4.   What do you do if the item being cataloged has several parts and no collective title?

5.5.5.   How do you record scale if the information is not expressed as a representative fraction?

5.5.6.   If you create the representative fraction, what else must you place in the bibliographic record?

5.5.7.   In cataloging an item containing relief or other three-dimensional aspects, how do you record scale?

5.5.8.   What is a "neat line" on a map?

5.5.9.   How do you describe the extent of the item for an atlas?

5.5.10.   How are dimensions given for cartographic materials?

5.5.11.   What is the chief source of information for two-dimensional cartographic materials?

5.5.12.   What is the chief source of information for three-dimensional cartographic materials?

5.5.13.   What is the general material designation (GMD) for cartographic materials?

5.5.14. If the item being cataloged consists of various physically separate parts, and no collective title exists, what should you do?

5.5.15. What do you do if there is no scale statement on the chief or prescribed sources of information?

5.5.16. What do you do if no scale can be determined?

5.5.17. When would you give a statement of projection?

5.5.18. If the item being cataloged is a globe containing only tactile data, how do you describe it in the 300 field?

5.5.19. What is the order of notes as prescribed by *AACR2R*?

5.5.20. What is the "recto" of a map?

5.5.21. How do you describe a collection of maps?

5.5.22.   What is the GMD for a collection of materials falling into both map and globe designations?

5.5.23.   When the item being cataloged is in a foreign language, do you use the language of the item in the 255 field?

5.5.24.   What do you do if the item being cataloged has several parts, and there are two scales given?

5.5.25.   What do you do if the item being cataloged has several parts, with three or more scales?

5.5.26.   What are the specific material designations (SMDs) used with cartographic materials?

5.5.27.   What do you do for a specific material designation if the item being cataloged is not one of the terms in the list in question 5.5.26?

5.5.28.   What are the "other physical details" used in the subfield b of the 300 field?

5.5.29.   When do you use an audience note in the bibliographic record for a map?

5.5.30. Do you include an ISBN or ISSN in the bibliographic record for a cartographic item?

5.5.31. What do you do if the item has no title?

5.5.32. What do you do if the location of the cartographic material is not given in the title?

5.5.33. How is "scale" expressed in the 255 field?

5.5.34. How do you express scale for celestial charts, maps of imaginary places, and maps with nonlinear scales?

5.5.35. How do you describe an item printed in two or more segments designed to fit together to form one or more maps?

5.5.36. What do you do if the item being cataloged is printed on something other than paper?

6.

KITS

Now you come to the fun part. Kits are easy to catalog because the bibliographic records for them are rather skimpy. A *kit* is defined as a collection of two or more types of media, none of which can be considered predominant. For example, a kit might consist of one videorecording, one carousel of eighty slides, six paperback books, a script of a play, several three-dimensional objects, and a manual. A filmstrip and cassette set, for example, is NOT a kit, because the filmstrip is considered predominant.

There may be several notes in the bibliographic record dealing with the various parts of the kit—titles and authors of the various parts, intellectual level, varying copyright dates, and so on. The physical description is usually a listing of all the components of the kit, in one long list. There are usually a summary, subject headings, and added title entries. In all, bibliographic records for kits may be quite a bit shorter than those for other formats.

6.1. Kits, Full Records Tagging Exercises

Add the proper tags, indicators, and subfields to the bibliographic records given here. The blanks indicate where tags, indicators, and subfields should be placed. Precede each subfield code with a delimiter. You will need to use the USMARC bibliographic formats, *AACR2R*, *LCSH*, and other tools.

6.1.1.   245 _ _   ____ Kinderkit ____ [kit] : ____ kindergarten.

260   ____ LaSalle, Ill. : ____ Open Court, ____ c1989.

300   ____ 1 set activity sheets, 2 sets of masters, 1 brown bear puppet, 1 record, 1 booklet, 1 cassette, 1 set of picture cards, 2 books, 1 set of wall cards, 1 set individual cards (4 copies), 1 set of flash cards (4 copies), 1 picture pack, 1 set of color cards, 1 set of shape cards.

440 _   ____ Open Court reading and writing

500   ____ Designed to be used with First star readiness teacher's guide in the Open Court reading and writing program.

520   ____ Teaches the alphabet in introducing the student to reading.

650 _   ____ Reading (Primary)

650 _   ____ Alphabet ____ Study and teaching (Primary)

650 _   ____ English language ____ Alphabet ____ Study and teaching (Primary)

6.1.2. 245 _ _   ____ Environments ____ [kit].

260   ____ New York : ____ Scholastic, ____ 1991.

300   ____ 1 sound cassette, 9 song charts, 1 paperback book (6 copies), 1 teaching plan, 1 banner.

440 _   ____ Scholastic banners

500   ____ Paperback book is entitled Earth songs, by Myra Cohn Livingston, poet, and Leonard Everett Fisher, painter.

500   ____ Sound cassette contains songs focusing on environmental concerns and interests.

520   ____ Uses a variety of materials to develop a program focusing on the environment.

650 _   ____ Habitat (Ecology)

650 _   ____ Ecology.

700 _   ____ Livingston, Myra Cohn. ____ Earth songs.

6.1.3. 2_ _ _   ____ SCREEN ____ [kit] : ____ screening children for related early educational needs / ____ Wayne P. Hresko ... [et al.].

2_ _ _   ____ Screening children for related early educational needs.

2_   ____ Austin, Tex. : ____ Pro-Ed, ____ c1988.

3_   ____ 1 profile/record form (25 copies), 1 student workbook (25 copies), 1 picture book, l examiner's manual, in container 17 × 26 × 3 cm.

5_   ____ Developed by Wayne P. Hresko, D. Kim Reid, Donald D. Hammill, Herbert P. Ginsburg, Arthur J. Baroody.

5_   ____ A measure of early academic proficiencies in the areas of oral language, reading, writing, and mathematics. Standardized research tool for early childhood programs that complies with standards of the American Psychological Association. For children ages 3-7. Useful for identifying mildly handicapped students.

6_ _   ____ Mentally handicapped children ____ Ability testing.

6_ _   ____ Learning ability ____ Testing.

6_ _   ____ Early Learning Skills Analysis.

6_ _   ____ Early childhood education ____ Activity programs.

6_ _   ____ Educational tests and measurements.

6_ _   ____ Preschool children ____ Ability testing.

7_ _   ____ Hresko, Wayne P.

6.1.4. 2_ _ _   ____ Algebra ____ [kit]

2_   ____ Glenview, Ill. : ____ Scott Foresman, ____ c1996.

3__   ____ 1 activity sourcebook, 1 geometry template, 8 overhead transparencies, 1 clear vinyl case (24 x 31 cm.)

5__   ____ "University of Chicago School Mathematics Project"

5__   ____ "The Activity Sourcebook is a collection of activities in blackline-master form accompanied by Teacher's notes designed to provide options in the teaching of lessons in UCSMP Algebra. The Activity kit includes eight overhead transparencies that aid in classroom discussion of the activities."--Introduction.

6__ _   ____ Algebra ____ Study and teaching.

7__ _   ____ University of Chicago. ____ School Mathematics Project.

6.1.5.   1__ _   ____ Erickson, Lynn Martin.

2__ _ _   ____ Remembering birthdays ____ [kit] / ____ by Lynn Martin Erickson and Kathryn Leide.

2__   ____ Madison, Wisc. : ____ Bi-Folkal Productions, ____ 1982.

3__   ____ 1 videocassette, 1 sound cassette, 1 program manual (2 copies), 1 booklet (Happy birthday), 1 booklet (Many happy returns) (25 copies), 2 graphics masters, 4 skit scripts (3 copies of each), 1 booklet (According to astrology) (25 copies) and 1 bag containing cake decorating tips, 2 candle holders, and an introduction to antique birthday cards, in canvas carryall.

5__   ____ Title from data sheet.

5__   ____ Designed to assist program leaders who work with groups of mentally alert older people in evoking memories of birthdays.

6__ _   ____ Birthdays.

7__ _   ____ Leide, Kathryn.

6.1.6.   2__ _ _   ____ Reminiscing ____ [kit] : ____ the game for people over thirty.

2__   ____ Glendale Heights, IL : ____ TDC Games, ____ 1989.

3__   ____ 1 game (17 pieces), 1 game/score board, 1 reminiscing booklet, 3 dice, 4 decade booklets, 8 pawns, in container 46 x 19 x 8 cm.

5__   ____ For 2 to 4 players or teams.

5__   ____ Intended audience: persons over thirty years of age.

5__   ____ Takes you through the years 1939-1979.

6__ _   ____ Memories.

6__ _   ____ Games. ____ lcsh

6.1.7.   ___ _ _   ____ Mathematics ____ [kit] : ____ exploring your world.

___   ____ Morristown, N.J. : ____ Silver Burdett & Ginn, ____ c1995.

___   ____ 9 kits containing overhead transparencies, manipulative connection cards, test booklets, home school connection booklets, and teacher editions of Applying my skills booklets, authentic assessment booklets, chapter support materials files, answer key booklets.

___   ____ 7 kits (grades K, 1, 2, 3, 4, 6, 7) in tote bags 34 × 36 × 12 cm. ; 2 kits (grades 5, 8) in tote bags 64 × 56 × 9 cm.

___   ____ Kits for Grades K-2 do not contain overhead transparencies.

___ _ ____ Mathematics ____ Study and teaching (Elementary)

___ _ ____ Arithmetic ____ Study and teaching (Elementary)

This one is all yours—no help, no tips, no blanks. Good luck.

6.1.8.   ___ _ _   [Game pieces] [kit].

___   [Atlanta, Ga. : Play Rugs Corp., 1967].

___   2 rings, 1 pole, 24 checkers (12 red, 12 black), 60 marbles (10 each red, orange, blue, green, purple, black), 4 horseshoes (plastic), 2 poles, 32 chess pieces (16 black, 16 red) in box 28 × 28 × 22 cm.

___   Title supplied by cataloger.

___   Designed to be used with game boards printed into a rug to be used in a recreation room.

___ _ Games.

___ _ Board games.

6.2. Kits, Error Identification Exercises

The number of errors in each record is given in parentheses at the top of the record. Find the errors and circle them. Write the corrections above the errors. The errors may be in spelling, tags, indicators, subfields, punctuation, etc.

6.2.1. (18 errors)

245 10   Reminiscence ≠h [kit] : ≠b finding meaning in meomries : ≠b training guide.

260   ≠a Wasington D.C. : ≠b Social Outreach and Support Section, Pogram Dept.,

American Association of Retired People, ≠c c1997.

300   ≠a 80 col. Slides, 1 sound cassette, 6 identical training guides, 1 slide show script, 1 resource materials booklet, and 2 leaflets ; + ≠e in binder 30 cm.

500   Title from binder.

500   ≠a Title of slide presentation: Memories, keys to the presnet.

505   ≠a Training guide for those working with the elderly and trying to use memories to give new meaning to their present day lives.

650 0   ≠a Childhood memories.

710 20   ≠a American Association of Retired Persons. Program Dept. Social Outreach and Support Section.

740 01   ≠a Finding meaning in memories.

740 10   ≠a Memories, keys to the present.

6.2.2. (9 errors)

245 10   ≠a Mathematics ≠h [activity kit] : ≠b manipulative activity kit.

260   ≠a White Plains, NY : Cuisenaire Company of America, c[1997?]

300   ≠a 411 color tiles -- 600 snap cubes -- 72 color dice -- 12 number cubes -- 15 counter bowls -- 15 decks of playing cards -- 2 menu posters, in container 65 × 12 × 36 cm.

500   ≠a For grades 1-2.

500   ≠a Title from container.

650 0   ≠a Mathematics ≠x Study and teaching (Grades 1, 2)

650 0   ≠a Seatwork and activities.

6.2.3. (10 errors)

100 1   ≠a Charles, Linda.

240 00   ≠a Mathland ≠h [kit] : ≠b journeys through mathematics. ≠p Grade 1 / ≠a Linda Charles ... [et al.].

260   ≠a Muontain View, CA. : ≠b Creative Publications, ≠c c1998.

505 0   ≠a 1 guidebook, 1 resource manager, 1 assessment guide, 1 daily tune-ups, 1 skill power teacher's edition, 1 videocassette, 1 calculator, assorted supplementary materials, 1 arithmetwists, 1 arithmetwists reproducibles, 1 arithmetwists teacher's edition, 1 skill power, 1 skill power reproducibles, 1 bridges to home reproducibles, assorted consumable and/or manipulative materials, in box 46 × 65 × 51 cm.

520   ≠a Videocassette, A peek into Mathland, is an overview of the Mathland program, its goals and use of the components in the kit.

650 0   ≠a Math ≠x Study and teaching (Elementary).

6.2.4. (15 errors)

245 00   ≠a Remembering train rides. ≠h [KIT] / ≠c designed by Lynne Erickson and Kathryn Leide.

262   ≠a Madison : ≠b Bi-Folkal Productions, ≠b University of Wisconsin-Madison Library School, ≠c 1977.

301   ≠a 1 kit ; 30 × 38 × 12 in.

440 1   ≠a Media kit for the elderly

505 0   ≠a Cassettes: All aboard. Sing-along. Ballads -- Large-print song sheets: 500 miles. I've been workin' on the railroad. Sentimental journey (25 copies each) -- Large-print poem sheets: From a railway carriage. Travel (25 copies each) -- 8 cards of jokes -- Skit script (When is the train due?) (4 copies) -- 1 large-print newspaper -- Photocopied masters of large-print songs and poems, including the poem The vanishing depot -- Train paraphernalia: 1 Amtrak menu, 1977. 1 Super Chief menu, 1937. 1 railroad schedule. 1 Amtrak annual report. 1 grease pen.

500   ≠a "An L.S.C.A.-funded project through the Wisconsin Division for Library Services"--p. iv, program manual.

500   ≠a Provides materials to help evoke memories of train rides; designed for program leaders who work with groups of mentally alert elderly people.

651 0   ≠a Travel, Railroad.

650 0   ≠a Trains ≠x Miscellanea.

700 1   ≠a Erickson, Lynne Martin.

700 2   ≠a Kathryn Leide.

6.2.5. (11 errors)

110 1   ≠a Mongolia. ≠b Juulchin Tourist Commission.

245 14   ≠a Learn about Mongoliea ≠h [kit] / ≠c Juulchin Tourist Commission.

260   ≠a Ulaanbaatar, Mongolia. ≠p The Commission. ≠c 1998.

300   ≠n 1 "ger" model, 1 videocassette, various carvings of native Mongolian animals, 1 dictionary, 1 man's hat, 1 woman's hat, 2 sound cassettes,

15 photographs, 1 children's book in native Mongolian script, in container

38 × 62 × 18 cm.

500   ≠a Titel from container.

500   ≠a Designed as a promotional packet to be used by travel agents in America to

attract travelers to the world's most sparsely populated country.

651   ≠a People's Republic of Mongolia ≠x Description and travel.

6.2.6. (1 error)

100 1   ≠a Ferguson, Bobby.

245 10   ≠a [Travels to China] ≠h [kit] / ≠c Bobby Ferguson.

260   ≠a [S.l. : ≠b s.n.], c1991.

300   1 map, 120 slides in carousel, 1 laughing Buddha, 1 sandalwood fan, 1 silk

robe, 1 jade dragon, 1 pack of playing cards, 1 stuffed panda toy, 1 Mao

jacket, 2 sound cassettes, and 1 home videocassette.

500   ≠a Title supplied by cataloger.

520   ≠a Kit was created by the author from materials brought back from a trip to

China for the purpose of lecturing to elementary school children. The slides

were reproduced from photographs, and the videocassette had been filmed by

another member of the trip.

651 0   ≠a China ≠x Description and travel.

6.2.7. (10 errors)

245 00   ≠a Kindersay ≠h kit.

246 02   ≠a Early learning development curriculum.

262   ≠a Devon, Penns. : ≠b PRIMAK publications, ≠c c1987-1991.

301   ≠a 248 flash cards, 72 lesson envelopes, activities cards inside some lesson

envelopes, 1 conceptual language development book, 1 auditory discrimination

[sic] auditory memory book, l placement test book, numerical index to picture

file, 1 box of interactive materials, 7 envelopes of paper shapes, 2 charts, in

container 26 x 32 x 25 cm.

500   ≠x Title from container.

500   Each envelope of paper shapes contains a different color: red, purple, orange,

green, blue, yellow and white.

630 00   ≠a Language arts (Early childhood).

6.2.8. (10 errors)

245 00   ≠a Kindergarten basics in math. ≠h KIT.

260   ≠a Englewood Cliffs, N.J. : ≠b Scholastic, ≠c 1982.

300   ≠a 32 activity crds; 1 mini-guide; 12 parent component spirit masters

(1 each in English and Spanish); 1 worksheet book; 1 teaching guide, in box,

25 x 32 x 6 cm.

440 1   ≠a Scholastic early childhood program

500   ≠a Title on teaching guide: Mathematics.

530   ≠a Presents mathematical concepts and introduces mathematics skills in an

ordered sequence, from recognizing patterns to thinking logically.

650 0   ≠a Arithmetic ≠b Study and teaching (Primary)

740 01   ≠a Mathematics.

830 0   ≠a Scholastic early childhood program.

6.3. Kits, 008 (Header) Information

The codes given here are specifically for kits. Use them to create 008 fields for the records in the exercises following the codes.

00–05	Date entered on file; indicates the date the record was created; recorded in the pattern *yymmdd* (year/year/month/month/day/day).
06	Type of date/publication status. One-character code that categorizes the type of dates given in 008/07–10 (Date 1) and 008/11–14 (Date 2). For serials, 008/06 also indicates the publication status.

    (blank)—No dates given; B.C. date involved. Each character in fields 008/07–10 and 008/11–14 contains a blank (.).

    c—Serial item currently published. 008/07–10 contains the beginning date of publication; 008/11–14 contains 9999.

    d—Serial item ceased publication. 008/07–10 contains beginning date of publication; 008/11–14 contains ending date.

    e—Detailed date; 008/07–10 contains year and 008/11–14 contains month and day, recorded as *mmdd*.

    i—Inclusive dates of collection.

    k—Range of years of bulk of collection.

    m—Multiple dates; 008/07–10 usually contains the beginning date and 008/11–14 contains the ending date.

    n—Dates unknown; each position in 008/07–10 and 008/11–14 contains blanks.

    p—Date of distribution/release/issue and production/recording session when different.

    q—Questionable date; 008/07–10 contains the earliest possible date; 008/11–14 contains the latest possible date.

    r—Reprint/reissue date and original date; 008/07–10 contains the date of reproduction or reissue (i.e., the most current date) and 008/11–14 contains the date of the original, if known.

    s—Single known/probable date. 008/07–10 contains the date; 008/11–14 contains blanks.

    t—Publication date and copyright date.

    u—Serial status unknown. 008/07–10 contains the beginning date of publication; 008/11–14 contains 9999.

07–10	(Date 1)

    (blank)—Date element is not applicable.

    u—Date element is totally or partially unknown.

11–14	(Date 2)

    (blank)—Date element is not applicable.

    u—Date element is totally or partially unknown.

15–17   Place of publication, production, or execution. A two- or three-character code that indicates the place of publication, production, or execution. Two-character codes are left-justified and the unused position contains a blank. [Codes for the United States consist of the two-letter ZIP code abbreviation plus *u* for United States. New York, for example, would be coded *nyu*.] Unless otherwise specified, codes are always lower-case letters.

18–22   Undefined. Contains a blank (.) or fill character (|).

23   Form of item

    (blank)—None of the following

a—Microfilm

b—Microfiche

c—Microopaque

d—Large print

f—Braille

r—Regular print reproduction (eye-readable)

24–34   Undefined. Each contains a blank (.) or a fill character (|).

35–37   Language. A three-character code indicating the language of the item.

38   Modified record. A one-character code that indicates whether any data in a bibliographic record is a modification of information that appeared on the item being cataloged or that was intended to be included in the USMARC record. Codes are assigned a priority, and, when more than one code applies to the item, are recorded in the order of the following list.

    (blank)—Not modified.

d—Dashed-on information.

o—Completely romanized/printed in script.

s—Shortened. Some data omitted because the record would have exceeded the maximum length allowed by a particular system.

x—Missing characters. Characters could not be converted into machine-readable form due to character set limitations.

39   Cataloging source. A one-character code that indicates the creator of the original cataloging record. The NUC symbol or the name of the organization may be contained in subfield ≠a of field 040.

    (blank)—Library of Congress

a—National Agricultural Library

b—National Library of Medicine

c—Library of Congress cooperative cataloging program

d—Other sources [most libraries fall here]

n—Report to *New Serial Titles*

u—Unknown

Kits, 008 (Header) Information Exercises

6.3.1. Form of item

    a. ____ Microopaque

    b. ____ Braille

    c. ____ Eye-readable

    d. ____ Microfilm

    e. ____ Large print

    f. ____ Microfiche

    g. ____ None

6.3.2. Modified record

    a. ____ Dashed-on information

    b. ____ Shortened

    c. ____ Not modified

    d. ____ Missing characters

    e. ____ Printed in script

    f. ____ Romanized

6.3.3. Date types

    a. ____ Detailed date

    b. ____ Questionable date

    c. ____ Serial status unknown

    d. ____ Range of years of bulk of collection

    e. ____ B.C. date involved

    f. ____ Date of distribution and production date differ

6.4. Kits, *AACR2R* Chapter 3 Exercises

6.4.1. How does *AACR2R* define "kit"?

6.4.2. Which chapter of *AACR2R* would you use to describe kits?

6.4.3. What do you do if the item has a lot of small, different pieces?

6.4.4. What are the general material designations (GMDs) used for kits?

6.4.5. When creating a note about particular parts of the item, do you give them together in one note or separately in different notes?

6.4.6. How is a kit described in the physical description field? Give both ways in your answer.

7.

MISCELLANEOUS NONPRINT MATERIALS

7.1. Miscellaneous Nonprint, Full Records Tagging Exercises

Add the proper tags, indicators, and subfields to the bibliographic records given here. The blanks indicate where tags, indicators, and subfields should be placed. Precede each subfield code with a delimiter. You will need to use the USMARC bibliographic formats, *AACR2R*, *LCSH*, and other tools.

7.1.1. 245 _ _ ____ The treasures of Tutankhamen ____ [slide].

260 ____ New York : ____ Metropolitan Museum of Art, ____ c1976.

300 ____ 41 slides : ____ col. ; ____ 35 mm. + ____ 1 sound cassette.

500 ____ Sound accompaniment compatible with manual and automatic equipment.

520 ____ Objects from the tomb of Tutankhamen including statuettes, masks richly inlaid with jewels, and funerary jewelry and furniture. Narrative explains each, tells its use, and gives a little Egyptian history from the time of Tutankhamen.

600 _ _ ____ Tutankhamen, ____ King of Egypt ____ Tomb.

650 _ ____ Art objects, Egyptian ____ Exhibitions.

651 _ ____ Egypt ____ Antiquities ____ Exhibitions.

710 _ ____ Metropolitan Museum of Art (New York, N.Y.)

7.1.2. 245 _ _ ____ Remembering college ____ [kit].

260 ____ New York : ____ Bi-Folkal Productions, ____ 1992.

300 ____ 1 banner, 3 paperback books, 75 slides (in carousel), 3 art prints, 1 songbook (30 copies), 5 duplicating masters, 2 sound cassettes, and 1 videocassette, in bag 54 x 12 x 26 cm.

520 ____ Designed to be used in nursing homes and retirement homes to stimulate memories and discussions among older persons.

650 _ ____ Universities and colleges ____ Miscellanea.

7.1.3.   100 _   ____ Ormond, Mary Jane, ____ 1941-

245 _ _   ____ Houmas House ____ [art reproduction] / ____ Mary Jane
Ormond.

260   ____ New York : ____ New York Reprographics, ____ 1964.

300   ____ 1 art print : ____ col. ; ____ 43 × 72 cm. on sheet
53 × 82 cm.

500   ____ Reproduction of oil painting originally painted in 1962.

650 _   ____ Houmas House Plantation (La.)

7.1.4.   245 _ _   ____ Alaska ____ [motion picture].

250   ____ 2nd ed.

260   ____ Portland, Ore. : ____ Encounter Productions, ____ c1984.

300   ____ 1 film reel (30 min.) : ____ sd., col. ; ____ 16 mm.

440 _   ____ International travel guides

520   ____ Introduces viewers to Alaska's fascinating history and to such
scenic wonders as Mount McKinley and Glacier Bay.

651 _   ____ Alaska ____ Description and travel.

7.1.5.   100 _   ____ Lacey, Susan, ____ 1944-

245 _ _   ____ Body of evidence ____ [microform] / ____ by Susan Lee Lacey.

250   ____ 1st ed.

260   ____ New York : ____ Apron Books, ____ c1967.

300   ____ 166 p. ; ____ 22 cm.

500   ____ Includes bibliographical references (p. 164-166).

533   ____ Microfiche. ____ Belleville, N.C. : ____ Micrographico,
____ 1985. ____ 44 microfiches : positive ; 11 × 15 cm.

650   0   ____ Murder ____ New York (State) ____ New York ____ Case
studies.

BIBLIOGRAPHY

Ninety-nine percent of being thought a genius consists
of knowing who to ask for information!

—Trey Lewis, Director
Red River Parish Library

General Materials

ALA Glossary of Library and Information Science. Chicago: American Library Association, 1982.

Chan, Lois Mai. *Cataloging and Classification: An Introduction.* 2nd ed. New York: McGraw-Hill, 1994.

Chan, Lois Mai, et al. *Dewey Decimal Classification: A Practical Guide.* 2nd ed. rev. for *DDC 21.* Albany, N.Y.: OCLC Forest Press, 1996.

Downing, Mildred Harlow, and David H. Downing. *Introduction to Cataloging and Classification.* 6th ed., rev. and greatly enlarged in accordance with *AACR2R88* and *DDC20.* Jefferson, N.C.: McFarland, 1992.

Intner, Sheila S., and Jean Weihs. *Standard Cataloging for School and Public Libraries.* 2nd ed. Englewood, Colo.: Libraries Unlimited, 1996.

Rowley, Jennifer. *Organizing Knowledge: An Introduction to Information Retrieval.* 2nd ed. Brookfield, Vt.: Ashgate, 1992.

Saye, Jerry D., and Desretta V. McAllister-Harper. *Manheimer's Cataloging and Classification: A Workbook.* 3rd ed., rev. and expanded. New York: Marcel Dekker, 1991.

Wynar, Bohdan S. *Introduction to Cataloging and Classification.* 8th ed. Edited by Arlene G. Taylor. Englewood, Colo.: Libraries Unlimited, 1992.

Special Materials

Anglo-American Cataloguing Rules. 2nd ed., 1988 revision. Prepared under the direction of the Joint Steering Committee for Revision of AACR, a committee of: the American Library Association, the Australian Committee on Cataloguing, the British Library, the Canadian Committee on Cataloguing, the Library Association, the Library of Congress. Edited by Michael Gorman and Paul W. Winkler. Chicago: American Library Association, 1988.

Dreissen, Karen C., and Sheila A. Smyth. *A Library Manager's Guide to Physical Processing of Nonprint Materials.* Westport, Conn.: Greenwood Press, 1995.

Frost, Carolyn O. *Media Access and Organization.* Englewood, Colo.: Libraries Unlimited, 1989.

Library of Congress. Cataloging Policy and Support Office. *Library of Congress Subject Headings.* 20th ed. Washington, D.C.: Library of Congress, 1997.

Olson, Nancy B. *Audiovisual Material Glossary.* Dublin, Ohio: OCLC, 1988.

———. *Cataloging of Audiovisual Materials: A Manual Based on AACR2.* New 3rd ed. Edited by Sheila Intner and Edward Swanson. DeKalb, Ill.: Minnesota Scholarly Press, 1992.

Rogers, JoAnn V., with Jerry D. Saye. *Nonprint Cataloging for Multimedia Collections.* 2nd ed. Littleton, Colo.: Libraries Unlimited, 1987.

Sears List of Subject Headings. 16th ed. Edited by Joseph Miller. New York: H. W. Wilson, 1997.

Urbanski, Verna, with Bao Chu Chang and Bernard L. Karon. *Cataloging Unpublished Nonprint Materials: A Manual of Suggestions, Comments, and Examples.* Lake Crystal, Minn.: Soldier Creek Press, 1992.

Weihs, Jean, and Shirley Lewis. *Nonbook Materials: The Organization of Integrated Collections.* 3rd ed. Ottawa: Canadian Library Association, 1989.

Periodicals and Serials

Audiovisual Librarian. London: Audiovisual Group of the Library Association, 1973– . Quarterly.

Cataloging & Classification Quarterly. Binghamton, N.Y.: Haworth Press, 1980– . Quarterly.

Cataloging Service Bulletin. Washington, D.C.: Library of Congress, 1978– . Quarterly.

Library Resources & Technical Services. Chicago: American Library Association, 1982– . Quarterly.

MOUG Newsletter. Cedar Falls, Iowa: Music OCLC Users Group, 1977– . Irregular.

Notes. Washington, D.C.: Music Library Association, 1943– . Quarterly.

OLAC Newsletter. Buffalo, N.Y.: OnLine Audiovisual Catalogers, 1981– . Quarterly.

Technical Services Quarterly. Binghamton, N.Y.: Haworth Press, 1983– . Quarterly.

Technicalities. Kansas City, Mo.: Media Services Publications, 1981– . Monthly.

Answer Key

1.3. General Nonprint Tagging Exercise Answers

Main Entries

1.3.1.	100 1	≠a Jones, Jessie.
1.3.2.	100 1	≠a Fitzgerald-Hughes, Edmund.
1.3.3.	110 1	≠a Utah. ≠b Legislature. ≠b House of Representatives.
1.3.4.	110 2	≠a Alabama Museum of Natural History.
1.3.5.	110 2	≠a Athabasca National Forest.
1.3.6.	100 1	≠a Petrovsky, Alexandrovitch, ≠d 1902-
1.3.7.	100 1	≠a Spears, John J. ≠q (John Julius), ≠d 1899-1942.
1.3.8.	100 0	≠a Timothy, ≠c of Jerusalem.
1.3.9.	110 2	≠a Bee Gees (Musical group)
1.3.10.	110 2	≠a Kansas City (Kans.). ≠b Police Jury.
1.3.11.	110 2	≠a Regional Planning Council for Southwest Louisiana.
1.3.12.	100 1	≠a Ford, Gerald R.
1.3.13.	100 1	≠a Pennywhistle, John, ≠c Sir, ≠d 1802-1901.
1.3.14.	111 2	≠a Monroe Bowling Tournament ≠d (1983 : ≠c Monroe, La.)

Title Statements

1.3.15.	245 0 0	≠a Faust ≠h [videorecording].
1.3.16.	245 1 4	≠a The body in the wall ≠h [sound recording] / ≠c Joe Boyd.
1.3.17.	245 1 0	≠a Sunny days ≠h [picture] / ≠c Elizabeth Crane.
1.3.18.	245 1 4	≠a The vampire companion ≠h [slide] / ≠c Anne Rice.
1.3.19.	245 1 5	≠a The "screech and howl" Halloween record ≠h [sound recording] / ≠c by the Screamers.
1.3.20.	245 1 4	≠a Niewe Amsterdamsegids ≠h [sound recording] = ≠b Guide to New Amsterdam / ≠c by E. de Rijk Spanhoff.
1.3.21.	245 1 0	≠a BASIC programming ≠h [computer file] / ≠c Nancy Davis.
1.3.22.	245 0 0	≠a Underneath the oceans of the world ≠h [globe].
1.3.23.	245 1 0	≠a Forest scenes ≠h [realia] / ≠c by Al Gore.
1.3.24.	245 1 0	≠a Fort Claiborne ≠h [map] / ≠c drawn by Cecil Atkinson.
1.3.25.	245 0 4	≠a The body in detail ≠h [model] / ≠c Will Tryon ... [et al.].
1.3.26.	245 1 0	≠a Family papers ≠h [microform] / ≠c Sir Matthew Hale.
1.3.27.	245 1 0	≠a Subtraction ≠h [flash card] / ≠c Chris Sharp.

Publication, Distribution, etc.

1.3.28.	260	≠a Englewood, Colo. : ≠b Libraries Unlimited, ≠c [1949].
1.3.29.	260	≠a Washington D.C. : ≠b U.S. Department of Education : [for sale by the U.S. G.P.O.], ≠c 1975.
1.3.30.	260	≠a London : ≠b Haynes ; ≠a Brookstone, Conn. : ≠b Auto Museum, ≠c c1997.
1.3.31.	260	≠a [Monterey, Mass.?] : ≠b Matthew Intner, ≠c 1986.
1.3.32.	260	≠a [Baton Rouge] : ≠b Louisiana State University Press, ≠c 1985.

Physical Description

1.3.33.	300	≠a 1 videodisc (35 min.) : ≠b sd., col., 1500 rpm ; ≠c 8 in.
1.3.34.	300	≠a 64 flash cards ; ≠c 22 × 10 cm.
1.3.35.	300	≠a 1 videorecording (65 min.) : ≠b sd., b&w ; ≠c ½ in.
1.3.36.	300	≠a 10 sound cassettes (15 hrs.) : ≠b mono.
1.3.37.	300	≠a 1 diorama (various pieces) : ≠b plywood and papier maché ; ≠c 18 × 28 × 12 cm.
1.3.38.	300	≠a 1 videocassette (22 min.) : ≠b sd., col. ; ≠c ½ in.
1.3.39.	300	≠a 1 microscope slide : ≠b glass ; ≠c 8 × 3 cm.
1.3.40.	300	≠a 1 game (15 pieces) : ≠b col., cardboard ; ≠c 9 × 12 in.
1.3.41.	300	≠a 1 sound disc (47 min.) : ≠b stereo. ; ≠c 12 in.
1.3.42.	300	≠a 2 film reels (60 min. ea.) : ≠b sd., b&w ; ≠c 16 mm.
1.3.43.	300	≠a 2 books, 1 carousel of slides, 3 transparencies, 2 workbooks (15 copies each), 1 guide (4 copies)
1.3.44.	300	≠a 1 score : ≠b 16 p. of music ; ≠c 28 cm.
1.3.45.	300	≠a 15 maps : ≠b col. ; ≠c 26-54 cm.
1.3.46.	300	≠a 1 sound disc (65 min.) : ≠b digital, stereo. ; ≠c 4 3/4 in.
1.3.47.	300	≠a 1 art reproduction : ≠b lithograph, col. ; ≠c image 33 × 41 cm., on sheet 46 × 57 cm.
1.3.48.	300	≠a 1 art original : ≠b pastel on paper ; ≠c 22 × 28 cm.

Series Statement

1.3.49.	440 _ 0	≠a Preservation guide
1.3.50.	490 0 _	≠a Fodor video guides
1.3.51.	410 2 _	≠a Nicholls State University. ≠b Center for Traditional Louisiana Boatbuilding. ≠t Wooden boat series
1.3.52.	490 0 _	≠a Electronic report / University of Southwestern Louisiana, Center for Archaeological Studies
1.3.53.	440 _ 0	≠a Water resources series. ≠n North Louisiana subseries

Notes

1.3.54.	500	≠a Title from disk label.
1.3.55.	520	≠a Summary: Shaquille O'Neal's greatest moves as a professional basketball player.
1.3.56.	501	≠a With: Only in your arms / Lisa Kleypas.
1.3.57.	504	≠a Includes discography (p. 547-569).
1.3.58.	500	≠a Title supplied by cataloger.
1.3.59.	500	≠a Videorecording of the motion picture from 1944.
1.3.60.	511	≠a Cast: Ronald Reagan, Bill Clinton, Richard Nixon.
1.3.61.	505 0	≠a Contents: Hey look me over -- Louisiana hayride -- Cajun two-step -- When the saints go marching in -- Bayou blues -- LSU alma mater.
1.3.62.	508	≠a Producers, Bill Gates and Bill Clinton ; music, Bill Conti ; screenplay, Bill Graham ; director, Bill Smith.
1.3.63.	500	≠a Includes 1 computer disk.
1.3.64.	500	≠a Includes subtitles in English.

Subject Descriptors

1.3.65.	600 1 0	≠a Nixon, Richard M.
1.3.66.	650 _ 0	≠a Gardening ≠z Louisiana ≠z New Orleans.
1.3.67.	610 2 0	≠a Louisiana. ≠b Office of the Lieutenant Governor.
1.3.68.	610 2 0	≠a State Library of Louisiana. ≠b Technical Services Branch.
1.3.69.	650 _ 0	≠a Cookery (Oysters)
1.3.70.	610 2 0	≠a Daughters of the Confederacy. ≠b Louisiana Chapter. ≠b Baton Rouge Post.
1.3.71.	651 _ 0	≠a Port Allen (La.) ≠x Politics and government.
1.3.72.	651 _ 0	≠a Alexandria (La.) ≠x History ≠y Civil War, 1861-1865.
1.3.73.	600 1 0	≠a Lawrence, Elizabeth, ≠d 1904-1985.
1.3.74.	650 _ 0	≠a Physically handicapped artists ≠z Louisiana.
1.3.75.	600 0 0	≠a Ferguson family.
1.3.76.	600 2 0	≠a Paul M. Hebert Law Center.
1.3.77.	651 _ 0	≠a Lafourche Parish (La.) ≠x Description and travel.
1.3.78.	610 1 0	≠a Lafayette Parish (La.). ≠b Office of the Mayor.
1.3.79.	620 2 0	≠a New Tickfaw Baptist Church (Livingston Parish, La.)
1.3.80.	600 0 0	≠a Joan, ≠c of Arc, Saint.
1.3.81.	651 _ 0	≠a Pilottown (La.) ≠x History.
1.3.82.	600 1 0	≠a Hunter, Bruce, ≠d 1958-
1.3.83.	651 _ 0	≠a East Feliciana Parish (La.) ≠x Economic aspects.
1.3.84.	650 _ 0	≠a Hurricanes ≠z Louisiana ≠z Cheniere Camanada.
1.3.85.	611 2 0	≠a Grand Isle Tarpon Rodeo ≠n (26th : ≠d 1979)
1.3.86.	630 0 0	≠a Bible. ≠p O.T. ≠p Genesis.

1.4. General Error Identification Exercise Answers

1.4.1. (̲1̲1̲0̲) 1   ≠a Smith, John, ≠d 1956-
  [above 110: 100]

1.4.2. (̲1̲3̲0̲) 1   ≠a Garcia Williams, John.
  [above 130: 100]

1.4.3. 110 (̲2̲)   ≠a Omaha (Neb.). ≠b Parish Council.
  [above 2: 1]

1.4.4. 100 (̲2̲)   ≠a Ann Margaret, ≠d 1943-
  [above 2: 0]

1.4.5. 111 (̲1̲)   ≠a Harpsichord championship ≠d (1995)
  [above 1: 2]

1.4.6. 245 (̲1̲0̲)   ≠a Solemn moments ≠h [sound recording].
  [above 10: 00]

1.4.7. (̲2̲4̲0̲ ̲1̲0̲)   ≠a The horse jumps ≠h [kit].
  [above 240 10: 245 04]

1.4.8. 245 10 (̲≠̲b̲) Everybody wins! ≠h [map] / ≠c Polly Tishan.
  [above ≠b: ≠a]

1.4.9. (̲2̲4̲6̲ ̲1̲4̲)   ≠a You @#$%^&*!!! ≠h [videorecording].
  [above 246 14: 245 00]

1.4.10. 245 (̲1̲2̲)   ≠a A man for all seasons ≠h [computer file].
  [above 12: 02]

1.4.11. 260   ≠a New York(: ≠b) c1996.
  [above : ≠b : ; ≠c]

1.4.12. 260   ≠a (⎯⎯⎯⎯⎯⎯) Libraries Unlimited, ≠c c1996.
  [above blank: Englewood, Co. : ≠b]

1.4.13. 260   ≠a Omaha, Neb. : ≠b Windy Press, (̲≠̲d̲) c1990.
  [above ≠d: ≠c]

1.4.14. 260 (̲0̲)   ≠a Gem, KS : ≠b J.W. Pub. Co., ≠c c1982.
  [above 0: [blank]]

1.4.15. 300   ≠a 1 map : (̲≠̲c̲) col. ; ≠c 22 × 18 cm.
  [above ≠c: ≠b]

1.4.16. 300   ≠a 54 slides : ≠b (̲s̲d̲) ; ≠c 35 cm.
  [above sd: col.]

1.4.17. 300   ≠a 1 doll : ≠b cloth ; ≠c 1965(̲-̲)
  [above -: .]

1.4.18. (̲3̲0̲1̲)   ≠a 1 puzzle (13 pieces) : ≠b wood, col. ; ≠c 25 cm.
  [above 301: 300]

2.1. Videorecordings, Full Records Tagging Exercise Answers

2.1.1.　245 0 0　≠a Seasons of crawfish culture ≠h [videorecording] / ≠c Cooperative Extension Service ; written and produced by Lynn E. Dellenbarger.

260　≠a [Baton Rouge : ≠b The Service?], ≠c 1991.

300　≠a 1 videocassette (22 min.) : ≠b sd., col. ; ≠c 1/2 in.

500　≠a "January 1991".

538　≠a VHS format.

520　≠a Lynn Dellenbarger, a professor at LSU working with shellfish in Ag Economics, discusses crawfish culture and its economic aspects. Also discusses how the Cooperative Extension Service can help improve results.

610 2 0　≠a Louisiana Cooperative Extension Service.

650 _ 0　≠a Crawfish ≠z Louisiana.

650 _ 0　≠a Agricultural extension work ≠z Louisiana.

700 1 _　≠a Dellenbarger, Lynn E. ≠q (Lynn Edwin), ≠d 1953-

710 2 _　≠a Louisiana Cooperative Extension Service.

2.1.2.　245 0 0　≠a Fish 'n' bloopers ≠h [videorecording] / ≠c Strike King Productions.

246 1 0　≠a Fishing bloopers.

260　≠a [S.l.] : ≠b Strike King Productions ; ≠a St.-Laurent, Quebec : ≠b Distributed by Madacy Music Group, ≠c c1993.

300　≠a 1 videocassette (ca. 40 min.) : ≠b sd., col. ; ≠c 1/2 in.

500　≠a "Recorded in EP mode."

500　≠a Closed captioned for the hearing impaired.

500　≠a "BDO-3-4306"

511　≠a Starring Bill Dance.

520　≠a Contains outtakes from the television series "Bill Dance Outdoors" and "Unforgettable moments" with some of his special guests, including Hank Williams, Jr., Mel Tillis, Bobby Goldsboro, Terry Bradshaw, and others.

538　≠a VHS format.

650 _ 0　≠a Fishing ≠x Humor.

700 1　≠a Dance, Bill.

2.1.3.　245 0 0　≠a Household consumption patterns for Louisiana crawfish ≠h [videorecording] / ≠c by Alvin Schopp and Lynn Dellenbarger.

260　≠a [Baton Rouge] : ≠b Louisiana Agricultural Experiment Station, ≠c 1993.

300　≠a 1 videocassette (21 min.) : ≠b sd., col. ; ≠c 1/2 in.

440 _ 0　≠a A.E.A. video information series

500　≠a "May 1993".

538　≠a VHS format.

500　≠a Title from videocassette label.

	520	≠a A lecture about how much crawfish Louisianians eat, where they get it, and special ways of cooking it.
	650 _ 0	≠a Crayfish.
	650 _ 0	≠a Crayfish ≠x Marketing.
	650 _ 0	≠a Cookery (Crayfish)
	700 1	≠a Schopp, Alvin.
	700 1	≠a Dellenbarger, Lynn E. ≠q (Lynn Edwin), ≠d 1953-
	710 2	≠a Louisiana Agricultural Experiment Station.
2.1.4.	130 0	≠a Short story in Louisiana.
	245 1 0	≠a The short story in Louisiana ≠h [videocassette] / ≠c edited by Mary Dell Fletcher.
	250	≠a 4th ed.
	260	≠a Lafayette, La. : ≠b Center for Louisiana Studies, University of Southwestern Louisiana, ≠c c1993.
	300	≠a 1 videocassette (20 min.) : ≠b sd., col./b&w ; ≠c 1/2 in.
	538	≠a VHS format.
	520	≠a A brief history of Louisiana short stories and the men and women who wrote them.
	650 _ 0	≠a Short stories, American ≠z Louisiana.
	651 _ 0	≠a Louisiana ≠x Fiction.
	700 1	≠a Fletcher, Mary Dell.
2.1.5.	110 2	≠a Treasures of the Kingdom (Krewe).
	245 1 0	≠a 1994 Mardi Gras ball ≠h [videorecording].
	260	≠a Lafayette, La. : ≠b Treasures of the Kingdom, ≠c c1994.
	300	≠a 1 videocassette (120 min.) : ≠b sd., col. ; ≠c 1/2 in.
	500	≠a Videographed by members of the Krewe.
	538	≠a VHS format.
	520	≠a Various members of the Lafayette Mardi Gras krewe videotaped their ball. Included are presentation of the court, entertainment by the Beach Boys, and costumes of the krewe members as the members of the Krewe danced.
	650 _ 0	≠a Carnival ≠z Louisiana ≠z Lafayette.
	650 _ 0	≠a Costume ≠z Louisiana ≠z Lafayette.
2.1.6.	100 1	≠a Ferguson, Bobby.
	245 1 0	≠a Travel and adventure in Outer Mongolia ≠h [videorecording] / ≠c Bobby Ferguson.
	246 1 0	≠a Outer Mongolia.
	260	≠c 1995.
	300	≠a 1 videocassette (60 min.) : ≠b sd., col. ; ≠c 1/2 in.
	538	≠a VHS format.
	520	≠a Bobby Ferguson videotaped her travels in Mongolia. Includes scenes from Ulaanbaatar, a nomad's ger (tent), Yoln Valley, the National Library of Mongolia, Gobi Desert, and much more.
	651 _ 0	≠a Mongolia ≠x Description and travel.
	651 _ 0	≠a Gobi Desert.
	650 _ 0	≠a Voyages and travels.

2.1.7.   245 0 0   ≠a Trees in Baton Rouge ≠h [videorecording].

246 1 0   ≠a Baton Rouge trees, a guide to the city.

250   ≠a 1st ed.

260   ≠a Baton Rouge : ≠b Louisiana Association of Nurserymen, ≠c 1994.

300   ≠a 1 videocassette (30 min.) : ≠b sd., col. ; ≠c 1/2 in.

500   ≠a Project supported by an America the Beautiful grant from the Louisiana Dept. of Agriculture.

500   ≠a Title on label: Baton Rouge trees, a guide to the city.

538   ≠a VHS format.

520   ≠a Includes specific subdivisions, specific trees, and tips for planting and growing exotic specimens.

650 _ 0   ≠a Trees in cities ≠x Law and legislation ≠z Louisiana.

710 2   ≠a Louisiana Association of Nurserymen.

2.1.8.   100 1   ≠a Guillory, Vincent.

245 1 0   ≠a An evaluation of escape rings in blue crab traps ≠h [videorecording] / ≠c by Vincent Guillory, Jerry Merrell.

260   ≠a Bourg, La. : ≠b Marine Fisheries Division, Louisiana Dept. of Wildlife and Fisheries, ≠c 1993.

300   ≠a 1 videocassette (15 min.) : ≠b sd., col. ; ≠c 1/2 in.

440 _ 0   ≠a A.E.A. video technical bulletin

538   ≠a VHS format.

520   ≠a A taped lecture on trapping blue crabs.

650 _ 0   ≠a Blue crabs.

650 _ 0   ≠a Crab fisheries ≠z Louisiana.

700 1   ≠a Merrell, Jerry.

710 1   ≠a Louisiana. ≠b Marine Fisheries Division.

2.2. Videorecordings, Notes Exercise Answers

Bayou passions

8
9
6
3
2
5
7
4
1

2.3. Videorecordings, Error Identification Exercise Answers

2.3.1. (14 errors)

```
      00                              ≠h
245 (04)   ≠a Christmas in America ( ) [videorecording].
```

```
   [blank]              ≠b
260 (0)   ≠a New York : (≠a) Hyper Press, ≠c c1995.
```

```
          ≠a    videocassette          1/2 in.
300   (≠t) 1 (videorecording) : ≠b sd., col. ; ≠c (16 mm.)
```

```
440                    [blank]
(400) 0   ≠a Holiday series (.)
```

```
511
(500)   ≠a Narrated by David Wines.
```

```
538
(500)   ≠a VHS format.
```

```
650                    ≠z
(651) 0   ≠a Christmas (≠x) United States.
```

```
      1_
700 (20)   ≠a Wines, David.
```

2.3.2. (8 errors)

```
      04                              [videorecording]
245 (00)   ≠a The Scottish are coming! ≠h (videorecording).
```

```
   [blanks]              (120 min.)
300 (00)   ≠a 2 videocassettes (≠t 120 min.) : ≠b sd., col. ; ≠c 1/2 in.
```

```
520        [delete Summary:]                program
(500)   ≠a  (Summary:)  Rehearsal of the (programmed) which the Scottish Black
        Watch Drum and Bugle Corps is planning to take on a world tour.
```

```
          ≠a
610 20   (≠ca) Scottish Black Watch Drum and Bugle Corps.
```

2.3.3. (14 errors)

```
      1_                    ≠d
100 (10)   ≠a White, Ronald, (≠a) 1944-
```

10   [videorecording]

245 ⑪ ≠a "How-to" on bodywork ≠h ([videocassette]) : car

                ≠c

refinishing / (≠a) SharpWhite Productions.

              Baton Rouge,

260   ≠a (B.R.,) LA : ≠b SharpWhite Productions, ≠c 1987.

        ≠a *[extent]* : ≠b *[other details]*, ≠c *[size]*.

300   (≠a : ≠b, ≠c)

520   demonstrate

⑤⑪ ≠a Ronnie White and Sam Sharp (demstrate) how to get rid of bumps, lumps, scratches, and dents in this absorbing demonstration of bodywork with an Austin-Healy Sprite.

650   ≠a   ≠x

⑥⑤⑪ 0 ◯ Automobiles (≠a) Refinishing.

700 1_

(710 20) ≠a White, Ronald, ≠d 1944-

700 1_

(710 20) ≠a Sharp, Sam, ≠d 1943-

2.3.4. (11 errors)

00   [videorecording]

245 ⑩ ≠a Handling firearms ≠h ([motion picture]).

260

(250)   ≠a Schiller Park, Ill. : ≠b MTI Teleprograms, ≠c c1979.

           videocassette

300   ≠a 1 (videorecording) (32 min.) : ≠b sd., col. ; ≠c 1/2 in.

508   ≠a

⑤⑪ (≠C) Production manager and special effects, Ron Adams ; director, Dennis Anderson ; script, Charles Remsberg.

520   techniques

(505 0) ≠a Covers the total range of (tecknicques) for safe handling of firearms. Shows how to prevent accidental discharge, malfunction, and unintentional hits. Discusses the consequences of wrong or faulty ammunition for law enforcement personnel.

650 0   ≠x

(651 1) ≠a Firearms (≠a) Safety measures.

          Police

650 0 ≠a (Police officer) training.

2.3.5. (14 errors)

```
        00      ≠a              ≠h
245 (04)  (  ) Enemy alien (≠a) [videorecording] / ≠c National Film Board of Canada.

250
(246)     ≠a 2nd ed.

                                    c1975
260       ≠a [Quebec, Ont.] : ≠b The Board, ≠c (c1795) .

          1                          , col.
300       ≠a (3) videocassette (25 min.) : ≠b sd. (  ) ; ≠c 1/2 in.

511
(508)     ≠a Narrator: Stanley Jackson.

508
(511)     ≠a Producer, Wolf Koenig ; director, Jeanette Lerman ; music, Eldon Rathbone.

                              internment
520       ≠a A documentary on Japanese (internal) during the Second World War.

          0                    ≠x
650  (4)  ≠a Japanese-Americans (≠y) Evacuation and relocation.

710 2_                        Canada
(700 10)  ≠a National Film Board of (Quebec) .
```

2.3.6. (13 errors)

```
          ≠a                            ≠h [videorecording]
245 00  (≠t) Computers and the quality of life ( ) / ≠c Regional
          Television Production Center, Moorhead State College.

          Moorhead,                    ≠c
260       ≠a (Moosehead,) Minn.  : ≠b The Center, (≠cc) p1973.

300               33
(301)     ≠a 1 videocassette ( (3333) min.) : ≠b sd., col.; ≠c 1/2 in.

440 _0  ≠a                              ≠v
(400 0) (≠t) Communicating about computers to the educator ; (≠n) no. 6

538       VHS
(500)     ≠a (VSH) format.
```

Discusses
520   ≠a (Discussion) why the computer is a powerful social device, whether or not a computer can "think", and whether or not the computer enhances creativity.

650 _0
(600 5) ≠a Computers.

2.3.7. (13 errors)

≠h videorecording   ≠b
245 00   ≠a In praise of hands (≠videorecording) = ( ) Hommage aux mains.

Hommage
246 10   ≠a (Frommage) aux mains.

Ont.
260   ≠a Quebec, (Canada) : ≠b National Film Board of Canada, ≠c 1974.

videocassette ([##] min.)
300   ≠a 1 (film reel (video)) : ≠b sd., col. ; ≠c 1/2 in.

538   VHS
(508)   ≠a (Vhs) format.

500   hearing
(538)   ≠a Closed captioned for the (visually) impaired.

520   Mexico
(522)   ≠a Shows people in various countries, including Japan, Nigeria, (Mehico) and Poland
(Pland) as they use their hands in creating works of craftsmanship.

650 0   ≠a Handicraft.

650 0
(655 7) ≠a Decorative arts.

2.3.8. (1 error)

CA
260   ≠a Universal City, (CAL) : ≠b Universal Pictures, ≠c 1978.

2.4. Videorecordings, 008 (Header) Information Exercise Answers

2.4.1.	Running time	
	a.	025
	b.	120
	c.	11
	d.	000
	e.	025
2.4.2.	Target audience	
	a.	c
	b.	b
	c.	e
	d.	g
	e.	a
	f.	d
	g.	f
	h.	j
	i.	b
2.4.3.	Accompanying matter	
	a.	oqs
	b.	lr
	c.	mrz
	d.	
	e.	qz
2.4.4.	Government publications	
	a.	l
	b.	f
	c.	s
	d.	i
	e.	
	f.	c
	g.	m
2.4.5.	Type of visual material	
	a.	o
	b.	f
	c.	w
	d.	g
	e.	m
	f.	l
	g.	a
	h.	t

2.4.6.   Technique
   a.   l
   b.   u
   c.   z
   d.   a
   e.   z

2.4.7.   970818s1996 . . . . nyu023 . e . . . . vleng . d
2.4.8.   970818s1997 . . . . nyu056 . e . . . . vzeng . d
2.4.9.   970818s1997 . . . . msu042 . dr . . . . s . . . . vzeng . d
2.4.10. 970818s1995 . . . . nyu051 . c . . . . vleng . d
2.4.11. 970818s1996 . . . . ohu030 . e . . . . vzeng . d
2.4.12. 970818s1997 . . . . fr . 093 . c . . . . vlfre . d
2.4.13. 970818s1993 . . . . utu043 . g . . . . vleng . d
2.4.14. 970818s1997 . . . . ilu030 . b . . . . vleng . d

2.5. Videorecordings, *AACR2R* Chapter 7 Exercise Answers

2.5.1.   (a) The item itself (the title frames), or (b) its container (and container label) if the container is an integral part of the piece (e.g., a cassette).

2.5.2.   Supply one as instructed in 1.1B7.

2.5.3.   Immediately after the first part of the title proper, before the equals sign.

2.5.4.   Either describe the item as a unit or make a separate description for each separately titled part.

2.5.5.   It can be given optionally, in addition to the publisher, if so desired.

2.5.6.   Yes, if the cataloging agency feels that this information is important.

2.5.7.   If the playing time is stated on the item, give it as stated. If not stated, do not give a playing time. Optionally, give the number of frames if readily ascertainable.

2.5.8.   If it is considered important, or if it is standard for the item.

2.5.9.   Yes.

2.5.10. Accompanying textual material (e.g., scripts, shot lists, publicity material), container (if not an integral part of the piece), or other sources.

2.5.11. Use a supplied title and include all major elements present in the picture in order of their occurrence (e.g., place, date of event, date of shooting, personalities, and subjects).

2.5.12. Add the word [trailer] in square brackets as a subtitle after other title information.

2.5.13. In the edition statement. If the information is not on the chief source of information, enclose it in square brackets.

2.5.14. Add a statement of function as instructed in 1.4E, in square brackets, if more than one agency is involved or if the function of the agency is not clearly stated.

2.5.15. Videocartridge, videocassette, videodisc, videoreel.

2.5.16. Aspect ratio and special characeristics (motion pictures), sound characteristics, color, projection speed (motion pictures).

2.5.17.	Either, but inches are generally used.	
2.5.18.	7.0C.	
2.5.19.	Immediately after the title proper.	
2.5.20.	Persons or bodies credited in the chief source of information with participation in the production, which are considered to be of major importance.	
2.5.21.	Transcribe the statement in the language or script of the title proper.	
2.5.22.	Use the date of the print being cataloged.	
2.5.23.	No. Give this information in a note.	
2.5.24.	Use the abbreviation "si." in subfield b.	
2.5.25.	No. Use the same form as for monographs.	
2.5.26.	Such information is always given in a note.	
2.5.27.	If the item contains parts belonging to materials falling into two or more categories, and if none of these is the predominant constituent of the item.	
2.5.28.	Yes.	
2.5.29.	Material (or type of publication) specific details area (Rule 7.3).	
2.5.30.	Use the date the item was created.	
2.5.31.	Immediately after the extent of item, subfield a.	
2.5.32.	Use b&w for sepia prints.	
2.5.33.	Nature or form; Language; Source of title proper; Variations in title; Parallel titles and other title information; Statements of responsibility; Edition and history; Publication, distribution, etc., and date; Physical description; Accompanying material; Series; Dissertations; Audience; Other formats; Summary; Contents; Unedited material and newsfilm; Numbers; Copy being described, library's holdings, and restrictions on use; "With" notes.	

3.1. Sound Recordings, Full Records Tagging Exercise Answers

3.1.1.	100 1	≠a O'Connor, Tony.
	245 10	≠a Uluru ≠h [sound recording] / ≠c Tony O'Connor.
	260	≠a Nambour, Qld., Australia : ≠b Studio Horizon Productions, ≠c [c1992].
	300	≠a 1 sound disc : ≠b digital, stereo. ; ≠c 4 3/4 in.
	505 0	≠a Freedom -- Valley of winds -- Mutitjula walk -- Dune -- Above with eagles -- Desert oak -- Touching sky -- Uluru.
	511	≠a Tony O'Connor, Paul Clement, Marshal Whyler.
	508	≠a Composed, arranged, and performed by Tony O'Connor ; production and direction by Jackie O'Connor.
	650 0	≠a Popular music ≠z Australia.
3.1.2.	100 1	≠a Kershaw, Doug.
	245 14	≠a The best of south Louisiana ≠h [sound recording] / ≠a Doug Kershaw and his band.
	260	≠a Baton Rouge, La. : ≠b Roll 'Em Productions, ≠c 1962.
	300	≠a 1 sound disc (80 min.) : ≠b digital, stereo. ; ≠c 4 3/4 in.
	500	≠a Compact disc.
	650 0	≠a Popular music ≠z Louisiana.

3.1.3.   100 1   ≠a McCaffrey, Anne.

245 10   ≠a Acorna, the unicorn girl ≠h [sound recording] / ≠c Anne McCaffrey and Margaret Ball.

260   ≠a New York : ≠b Harper Audiobooks, ≠c c1997.

300   ≠a 13 sound recordings (19.5 hrs.) : ≠b mono.

500   ≠a Unabridged.

511   ≠a Read by Sandra McIntyre-Colby.

520   ≠a When three miners find an escape pod with a live unicorn girl inside, they decide to adopt her and raise her themselves instead of letting her be mutilated and imprisoned by ambitious scientists.

650 0   ≠a Fantastic fiction. ≠2 gsafd

700 1   ≠a Ball, Margaret.

700 1   ≠a McIntyre-Colby, Sandra.

3.1.4.   100 1   ≠a Carter, Hodding, ≠d 1907-1972.

245 10   ≠a John Law wasn't so wrong ≠h [sound recording] / ≠c by Hodding Carter.

250   ≠a 1st ed.

260   ≠a Baton Rouge, La. : ≠b Esso Standard Oil Co., ≠c c1952.

300   ≠a 1 sound disk (20 min.) : ≠b 33 1/3 rpm, mono. ; ≠c 12 in.

511   ≠a Narrated by Edwin Edwards.

651 0   ≠a Louisiana ≠x Economic conditions.

651 0   ≠a Louisiana ≠x Industries.

700 1   ≠a Edwards, Edwin W.

3.1.5.   100 1   ≠a Wilds, John.

245 10   ≠a Alton Ochsner, surgeon of the South ≠a [sound recording] / ≠a John Wilds and Ira Harkey.

260   ≠a Baton Rouge : ≠b Louisiana State University Press, ≠c 1990.

300   ≠a 2 sound cassettes (120 min.) : ≠c mono.

511   ≠a Read by Ira Harkey.

600 10   ≠a Ochsner, Alton, ≠d 1896-

650 0   ≠a Surgeons ≠z Louisiana ≠x Biography.

700 1   ≠a Harkey, Ira, ≠d 1918-

3.1.6.   100 1   ≠a Lynn, Stuart M.

245 10   ≠a New Orleans ≠h [sound recording] / ≠c by Stuart M. Lynn.

260   ≠a New York : ≠b Hastings House Audio, ≠c 1949.

300   ≠a 1 sound disc (68 min.) : ≠b mono.

511   ≠a Read by Julie Aillet.

520   ≠a A tour of New Orleans giving historical information about various places in the Vieux Carré, or French Quarter, of New Orleans, Louisiana.

650 0   ≠a Vieux Carré (New Orleans, La.) ≠x Description and travel.

650 0   ≠a New Orleans (La.) ≠x History.

700 1   ≠a Aillet, Julie.

3.1.7.   245 00   ≠a By hand and by eye ≠h [sound recording] : ≠b South Louisiana wooden boat builders and their stories / ≠c Center for Traditional Louisiana Boatbuilding, Nicholls State University.

260   ≠a Thibodaux, La. : ≠b The Center, ≠c 1986.

300   ≠a 2 sound cassettes (120 min.) : ≠b mono.

440 0   ≠a Boat building oral history series

520   ≠a Four boatbuilders from south Louisiana tell the way they got into the boat building business and how each learned his trade.

650 0   ≠a Boatbuilding ≠z Louisiana.

651 0   ≠a Louisiana ≠x History, Local.

650 0   ≠a Oral history.

710 2   ≠a Nicholls State University. ≠b Center for Traditional Louisiana Boatbuilding.

3.1.8.   100 1   ≠a Connolly, John B.

245 10   ≠a Underway ≠h [sound recording] : ≠b tour of a tin can sailor / ≠c John B. Connolly.

246 10   ≠a Tour of a tin can sailor.

260   ≠a Baton Rouge, La. : ≠b J.B. Connolly, ≠c 1990.

300   ≠a 2 sound cassettes (150 min.) : ≠b mono.

500   ≠a Sold by subscription to raise money for the Veterans of Foreign Wars.

510   ≠a Read by the author, this cassette package gives the memoirs of J.B. Connolly's tour of duty as a member of the U.S. Navy during the Korean War.

600 10   ≠a Connolly, John B.

610 10   ≠a United States. ≠a Navy ≠a Biography.

650 0   ≠a Korean War, 1950-1953 ≠a Personal narratives, American.

3.2. Sound Recordings, Notes Exercise Answers

Christmas in the Holy Land

2
4
10
3
5
8
9
7
6
1

3.3. Sound Recordings, Error Identification Exercise Answers

3.3.1. (20 errors)

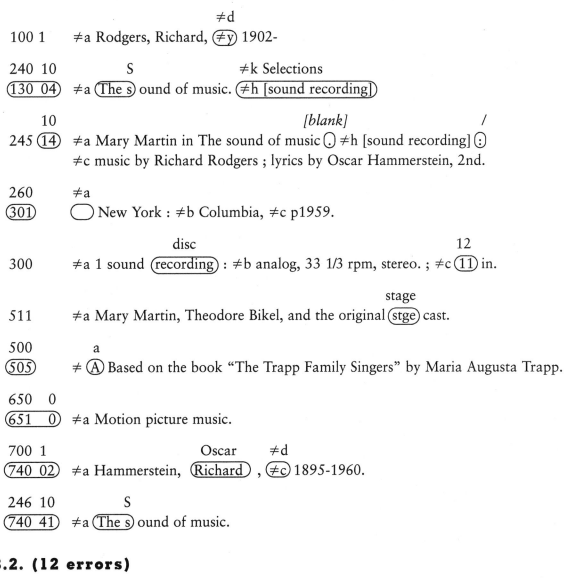

```
                              ≠d
100 1    ≠a Rodgers, Richard, (≠y) 1902-

240 10          S              ≠k Selections
(130 04)  ≠a (The s)ound of music. (≠h [sound recording])

        10                        [blank]                /
245 (14)  ≠a Mary Martin in The sound of music (.) ≠h [sound recording] (:)
          ≠c music by Richard Rodgers ; lyrics by Oscar Hammerstein, 2nd.

260      ≠a
(301)     ( ) New York : ≠b Columbia, ≠c p1959.

                   disc                              12
300      ≠a 1 sound (recording) : ≠b analog, 33 1/3 rpm, stereo. ; ≠c (11) in.

                                             stage
511      ≠a Mary Martin, Theodore Bikel, and the original (stge) cast.

500          a
(505)     ≠ (A) Based on the book "The Trapp Family Singers" by Maria Augusta Trapp.

650   0
(651   0)  ≠a Motion picture music.

700 1              Oscar    ≠d
(740 02)  ≠a Hammerstein, (Richard) , (≠c) 1895-1960.

246 10          S
(740 41)  ≠a (The s)ound of music.
```

3.3.2. (12 errors)

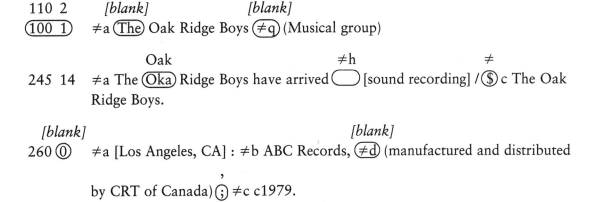

```
110 2    [blank]              [blank]
(100 1)   ≠a (The) Oak Ridge Boys (≠q) (Musical group)

         Oak              ≠h              ≠
245 14   ≠a The (Oka) Ridge Boys have arrived ( ) [sound recording] /(\$)c The Oak
         Ridge Boys.

   [blank]                        [blank]
260 (0)  ≠a [Los Angeles, CA] : ≠b ABC Records, (≠d) (manufactured and distributed
                      ,
         by CRT of Canada) (;) ≠c c1979.
```

	sound cassette
300	≠a 1 (audiocassette) (33 min.) : ≠b stereo.

508	
(511)	≠a Produced by Ron Chancey ; string and horn arrangements by Bergen White.

	Country music
650 0	(Popular music, Country style) .

3.3.3. (24 errors)

	1_ ≠d
100 (20)	≠a Shostakovich, Dmitrii Dmitrievich, (≠a) 1906-1975.

	10 ≠m
240 (14)	≠a Concertos, (≠a) violoncello, orchestra, ≠n no. 1, op. 107, ≠r E♭.

	≠a Concerto *[blank]*
245 10	(≠t) (Concertoe) for cello, in E flat, op. 107. (≠a) Symphony no. 1, in F major,
	≠h ≠c Shostakovich
	op. 10 ( ) [sound recording] / (Shostakovitch) .

	New York, N.Y.
260	≠a (New York City, New York) : ≠b Columbia, ≠c [1960?]

	disk : ≠b ; ≠c
300	≠a 1 sound (disc) (57 min.) ;(≠c) digital, stereo. ( ) 4 3/4 in.

	440 *[blank]*
(410) 0	≠a Columbia masterworks (.)

	511 violoncello
(508)	≠a Mstislav Rostropovich, (violonchello) ; Mason Jones, French horn ;
	Orchestra
	The Philadelphia (Orcestra) , Eugene Ormandy, conductor.

500	≠a Program notes on container.

	≠a
650 0	(≠t) Symphonies.

	_0 Concertos (Violoncello)
650 (0)	≠a (Violoncello concertos)

	700 1 Dmitrievich, ≠t
(740 02)	≠a Shostakovich, Dmitrii (D.) , ≠d 1906-1975. (≠x) Symphonies, ≠n no. 1, op. 10, ≠r F major.

3.3.4. (8 errors)

110 2   Captain   Musical
(110 1) ≠a (Captian) & Tennille ((Music) group)

                                 [sound recording]   ≠c
245 10   ≠a Love will keep us together ≠h (sound cassette) / (≠a) The Captain & Tennille.

           Beverly
260   ≠a (Beverley) Hills, Calif. : ≠b A&M Records, ≠c 1975.

                                                           12 in.
300   ≠a 1 sound disk (ca. 35 min.) : ≠b 33 1/3 rpm, stereo. ; ≠c (3 7/8 × 2 1/2 in.)

            Popular music
650 0   ≠a (Music, Popular (Songs, etc.)) ≠z United States.

3.3.5. (1 error)

                       61
300   ≠a 1 sound disk ((60.5) min.) : ≠b 33 1/3 rpm, stereo. ; ≠c 12 in.

3.3.6. (16 errors)

                     martyrs   ≠h [sound recording]   ≠
245 00   ≠a Fox's book of (marters) (   ) / (\)c edited by William B. Forbush.

260   Tenn.   c1969.
(262)   ≠a Nashville, (N.Y.) : ≠b Zondervan, ≠c (c1967, c1968, c1969) .

          10
300   ≠a (1) sound cassettes (15 hrs.) : ≠b mono.

           ≠a
511   (≠n) Read by Sir Robert Burns.

       _0   Persecution
650 (0)   ≠a (Persocution) ≠x Moral and ethical aspects.

                ≠x
650 0   ≠a Saints (≠z) Biography.

                ≠x
650 0   ≠a Martyrs (≠z) Biography.

       1   ≠d
700 (2)   ≠a Forbush, William Byron, (≠c) 1868-1927.

```
700                              ≠c
(720) 1      ≠a Burns, Robert, ◯ Sir.
```

3.3.7. (12 errors)

```
                 Urbanski
100 1    ≠a (Urbenski), Verna.

        10                                    sound recording
245 (04)   ≠a Cataloging unpublished nonprint materials ≠h (audio cassette)/
         ≠c by Verna Urbanski, principal author, with Bao Chu Chang and Bernard L.
                                 Swanson
         Karon ; edited by Edward (Svenson) .

             1st ed.
250      ≠a (First edition) .

                        Soldier
260      ≠a Lake Crystal, Minn. : ≠b (Solder) Creek Press, ≠c 1992.

                 cassette      mins.
300      ≠a 1 sound (recording) (120 (hrs.) )

511
(508)    ≠a Read by the author.

                 nonbook
650   0  ≠a Cataloging of (nonprint) materials.

630 00                  cataloguing
(650    0)  ≠a Anglo-American (cataloging) rules.
```

3.3.8. (10 errors)

```
700 1
(100 10)  ≠a Paul Newman.

                 ≠h
245 04   ≠a The sting (≠a) [sound recording] / ≠c Universal Pictures.

             Universal
260      ≠a (University) City, CA : ≠b Universal Pictures, ≠c 1988.
                                            12 in.
300      ≠a 1 sound disc (60 min.) : ≠b stereo. ; ≠c (3 7/8 in) .

500
(501)    ≠a Music from the motion picture by the same title.
```

511   Robert
(508)   ≠a Robert Redford, (Roert) Shaw, Paul Newman.

     1_
700 (21)   ≠a Redford, Robert.

     1_   Shaw
700 (21)   ≠a (Shawm), Robert.

3.4. Sound Recordings, 008 (Header) Information Exercise Answers

3.4.1.   Form of composition

      a.   <u>co</u>

      b.   <u>mz</u>

      c.   <u>ri</u>

      d.   <u>sy</u>

      e.   <u>uu</u>

      f.   <u>pr</u>

      g.   <u>mu</u>

      h.   <u>pt</u>

      i.   <u>df</u>

      j.   <u>sn</u>

3.4.2.   Format of music

      a.   <u>b</u>

      b.   <u>g</u>

      c.   <u>d</u>

      d.   <u>a</u>

      e.   <u>m</u>

      f.   <u>e</u>

      g.   <u>c</u>

      h.   <u>u</u>

      i.   <u>b</u>

3.4.3.   Target audience

      a.   <u>c</u>

      b.   <u>a</u>

      c.   <u>e</u>

      d.   <u>g</u>

      e.   <u>c</u>

3.4.4.   Form of item

    a.   <u> a </u>

    b.   <u> c </u>

    c.   <u> d </u>

    d.   <u> b </u>

    e.   <u> f </u>

    f.   <u> r </u>

    g.   <u>   </u>

3.4.5.   Accompanying matter

    a.   <u> bef </u>

    b.   <u>cdis</u>

    c.   <u> gh </u>

    d.   <u> ade </u>

    e.   <u> c </u>

    f.   <u>gikr</u>

    g.   <u>abd</u>

3.4.6.   Literary text

    a.   <u> b </u>

    b.   <u> e </u>

    c.   <u> c </u>

    d.   <u> a </u>

    e.   <u> f </u>

    f.   <u> m </u>

    g.   <u> t </u>

    h.   <u> o </u>

    i.   <u> l </u>

3.4.7.   008 . . . . . . s1996 . . . . nyufmn . g . . . . eng . d

3.4.8.   008 . . . . . . s1993 . . . . utunnn . e . . . . l . . . eng . d

3.4.9.   008 . . . . . . s1997 . . . . ilunnn . g . . . . mt . . . eng . d

3.4.10.   008 . . . . . . s1996 . . . . enknnn . g . . . . f . . . eng . d

3.4.11.   008 . . . . . . s1996 . . . . dcunnn . e . . . . e . . . eng . d

3.4.12.   008 . . . . . . s1996 . . . . mounnn . e . . . . h . . . eng . d

3.4.13.   008 . . . . . . s1997 . . . . akunnn . g . . . . h . . . eng . d

3.4.14.   008 . . . . . . s1971 . . . . xxusgn . g . . . . eng . d

3.5. Sound Recordings, *AACR2R* Chapter 6 Exercise Answers

3.5.1.   Discs, tapes (open reel-to-reel, cartridges, cassettes), piano rolls (and other rolls), and sound recordings on film, other than those intended to accompany visual images.

3.5.2.   Recordings in other forms, specifically wires and cylinders, or in various experimental media.

3.5.3.   Writers of spoken words, composers of performed music, and collectors of field material for sound recordings.

3.5.4.   Rule 1.1G3.

3.5.5.   Treat it as a series title.

3.5.6.   Give the fractional extent in the form "on side 3 of 4 sound discs", or "on reel 2 of 5 sound tape reels".

3.5.7.   Record the smallest and the largest separated by a hyphen.

3.5.8.   Yes.

3.5.9.   When it furnishes a collective title and the parts themselves and their labels do not.

3.5.10.   Put it in the note area.

3.5.11.   Take the presence of such words as *edition*, *issue*, or *version*, or their equivalent in other languages, as evidence that it is a different edition.

3.5.12.   Put it in a note.

3.5.13.   Type of recording, playing speed, groove characteristic (analog discs), track configuration (sound track films), number of tracks (tapes), number of sound channels, recording and reproduction characteristics.

3.5.14.   3 7/8 × 2 1/2 in., 1/8 in. tape.

3.5.15.   Sound recording.

3.5.16.   Give them in a note position if they are considered important; otherwise omit them.

3.5.17.   A noncommercial recording that generally exists in a unique copy.

3.5.18.   In the imprint field. As this item is unpublished, the date of recording is the date used.

3.5.19.   No.

3.5.20.   None.

3.5.21.   Immediately following the title proper.

3.5.22.   Either as a unit or with separate records for each titled part.

3.5.23.   Use the subordinate unit as the name of the publisher.

3.5.24.   Sound cartridge, sound cassette, sound disc, sound tape reel, and sound track film.

3.5.25.   Mono., stereo., quad.

3.5.26.   Nature or artistic form and medium of performance; Language; Source of title proper; Variations in title; Parallel titles and other title information; Statements of responsibility; Edition and history; Publication, distribution, etc.; Physical description; Accompanying material; Series; Dissertations; Audience; Other formats; Summary; Contents; Publishers' numbers; Copy being described, library's holdings, and restrictions on use; "With" notes.

4.1. Computer Files, Full Records Tagging Exercise Answers

4.1.1.   100 1   ≠a Lutus, Paul.

245 10   ≠a Musicomp ≠h [computer file] / ≠c by Paul Lutus.

246 10   ≠a Music comp.

256   ≠a Computer program (14 files)

260   ≠a Cupertino, Calif. : ≠b Apple Computer, Inc., ≠c c1980.

300   ≠a 1 computer disk : ≠b sd., col. ; ≠c 5 1/4 in. + ≠e 1 manual (22 p. ; 22 cm.)

440 0   ≠a Special delivery software

538   ≠a System requirements: Apple II or higher.

520   ≠a Uses the Apple's sound generating capability to play music and displays the musical notes on the screen as they are played. Also allows user to program his own compositions and add to the disk.

650 0   ≠a Composition (Music)

650 0   ≠a Music ≠x Computer-assisted instruction.

710 2   ≠a Apple Computer, Inc.

753   ≠a Apple II

4.1.2.   100 1   ≠a Williams, Robert.

245 10   ≠a Missing facts ≠h [computer file] / ≠c by Robert Williams.

246 10   ≠a Missing math facts.

260   ≠a Freeport, N.Y. : ≠b Educational Activities, ≠c c1980.

300   ≠a 1 computer disk : ≠b col. ; ≠c 5 1/4 in.

440 0   ≠a Mathematics series

538   ≠a System requirements: Apple II.

500   ≠a Also called: Missing math facts.

500   ≠a Copyright by Activity Records.

520   ≠a Includes examples for addition, subtraction, multiplication, and division with four levels of difficulty for each process.

650 0   ≠a Arithmetic ≠x Computer-assisted instruction.

710 2   ≠a Educational Activities (Firm)

710 2   ≠a Activity Records Inc.

753   ≠a Apple II.

4.1.3.   100 1   ≠a Roos, T. B.

245 10   ≠a Life+ ≠h [computer file] : ≠b life, death, and change / ≠c T.B. Roos.

246 10   ≠a Life, death, and change.

246 10   ≠a Life plus.

246 10   ≠a Biobits 1.

246 10   ≠a Biobits one.

246 10   ≠a Tribbles.

260   ≠a Wentworth, N.H. : ≠b COMPress, ≠c c1980.

300		≠a 1 computer disk : ≠b col. ; ≠c 5 1/4 in. + ≠e 1 manual and 1 Tribbles (student tutorial booklet).
538		≠a System requirements: Apple IIe.
500		≠a Title on guide: Biobits I: Life.
500		≠a Tribbles: An introduction to the scientific method / Ruth Von Blum and Thomas Mercer Hursh.
520		≠a Elements in a grid reproduce, maintain, or extinguish themselves according to a set of formal rules.
650	0	≠a Science ≠x Methodology.
700	1	≠a Von Blum, Ruth.
700	1	≠a Hursh, Thomas Mercer.
710	2	≠a COMPress (Firm)
753		≠a Apple IIe

4.1.4.

245	00	≠a Microreporter ≠h [computer file].
246	10	≠a PC reporter.
256		≠a Computer data (1 file : 800 records, 3150 bytes).
260		≠a New York : ≠b Simon & Schuster, ≠c c1992.
300		≠a 1 computer disk ; ≠c 3 1/2 in.
538		≠a System requirements: 386 system or higher; minimum 4 MB (8 MB recommended); Windows 3.0 or higher; hard drive; pen or stylus.
500		≠a Title from title screen.
500		≠a Title on disk label: PC reporter.
650	0	≠a Journalism ≠x Software.
753		≠a IBM compatible

4.1.5.

100	1	≠a Bergeron, Bryan P.
245	10	≠a Heartlab ≠h [computer file] : ≠b clinical cardiology auscultatory simulation / ≠c [Bryan P. Bergeron].
256		≠a Computer program.
260		≠a [S.l.] : ≠b B.P. Bergeron, ≠c c1988.
300		≠a 1 computer disk ; ≠c 3 1/2 in. + ≠e 1 guide (41 p.)
538		≠a System requirements: Macintosh 512, 512E, Plus, SE, or Macintosh II; 512K; Heartblock sound interface; miniature stereo headphones.
500		≠a Title from disk label.
500		≠a "Developed in the Decision Systems Group, Brigham & Women's Hospital, Harvard Medical School"--Guide.
500		≠a "Williams & Wilkins electronic media"--Guide.
650	0	≠a Heart ≠x Study and teaching ≠x Software.

4.1.6.

245	00	≠a Assessment of neuromotor dysfunction in infants ≠h [interactive multimedia] / ≠c produced by the Division of Developmental Disabilities, Dept. of Pediatrics, College of Medicine and Computer-Assisted Instruction Laboratory, Weeg Computing Center, the University of Iowa.

260 ≠a Baltimore : ≠b Williams & Wilkins, ≠c c1984.

300 ≠a 1 videodisc, 5 computer disks, 1 guide.

538 ≠a System requirements for videodisc: Pioneer LD-V6000 or compatible.

538 ≠a System requirements for computer disks: IBM PC or compatible; IBM InfoWindow System.

500 ≠a Title from cover of guide.

500 ≠a Title on videodisc label: Assessment of nevromotor [sic] dysfunction in infants.

508 ≠a Hosted by James A. Blackman, Loretta Knutson Lough, Joan Sustick Huntley.

500 ≠a Computer disks upgraded periodically.

500 ≠a "Williams & Wilkins electronic media"--Guide.

505 0 ≠a Assessment of neuromotor dysfunction in infants (version A) -- Pediatrics demo (automatic version) -- Pediatrics demo (non-automatic) -- Infant retrieval -- Assessment of neuromotor dysfunction in infants (version B).

650 0 ≠a Neurological disorders in infants ≠x Software.

710 2 ≠a University of Iowa. ≠b College of Pediatrics. ≠b Division of Developmental Disabilities.

4.1.7. 245 00 ≠a Medication administration ≠h [interactive multimedia] / ≠c [American Journal of Nursing Company ; produced by Thomas Jefferson University, Office of Academic Computing and the Department of Nursing, College of Allied Health Sciences].

260 ≠a [Philadelphia, Pa.] : ≠b Thomas Jefferson University, ≠c c1990-

300 ≠a videodiscs : ≠b sd., col. ; ≠c 12 in.

300 ≠a computer disks ; ≠c 3 1/2-5 1/4 in.

300 ≠a guides.

538 ≠a System requirements for videodiscs: videodisc player.

538 ≠a System requirements for computer disks: IBM PC or compatible; 640K (1 section requires 256K of graphics memory); DOS 3.3; InfoWindow Presentation System Interpreter, level 55; touch-screen monitor or M-Motion Video Adapter/A, EGA graphics display, 20MB hard disk.

500 ≠a Title from t.p. of module 1 guide.

500 ≠a Created by Sharon Renshaw, F. Scott Baedenkopf.

500 ≠a Issued with full set of computer disks in both sizes.

650 0 ≠a Pharmacopoeia ≠x Software.

710 2 ≠a Thomas Jefferson University. ≠b Office of Academic Computing.

710 2 ≠a Thomas Jefferson University. ≠b Dept. of Nursing.

4.1.8. 245 04 ≠a The American business disk ≠h [computer file].

246 10 ≠a Business for America.

250 ≠a Macintosh version.

260	≠a Omaha, Neb. : ≠b J. Smith, ≠c c1992.
300	≠a 1 computer disk : ≠b col. ; ≠c 3 1/2 in. + ≠e 2 computer discs and guide.
538	≠a System requirements: Macintosh System 7; VGA graphics card; 2 CD-ROM players.
500	≠a Version information from disk label.
500	≠a Title from title screen.
500	≠a Title on CD-ROM disks: Business for America.
650 0	≠a Business ≠x Software.
753	≠a Macintosh System 7

4.2. Computer Files, Notes Exercise Answers

Run to the White House

4
3
7
5
1
2
9
8
10
6

Computer animation

4
2
7
9
5
1
10
8
3
6

4.3. Computer Files, Error Identification Exercise Answers

4.3.1. (14 errors)

100
(101) 1   ≠a Zaron, E.

    10   ≠h
245 (40)   ≠a Super-text form letter module ◯ [computer file].

          ≠a
250   (≠v) Version 1.0

               Md.   [date]
260   ≠a Baltimore, (N.Y.) : ≠b Muse Software, ≠c (3 1/2 in.)

300   *[input physical description here]*
    ⬭

                                   [type of computer]
538   ≠a System requirements: (computer), printer.

                            title
504   ≠a Title from (titel) screen.

              ≠a
520   (≠Summary:) To be used with form letter file created using the program Super-text file, and address file created using Muse Address book program.

      _0   Commercial correspondence.
650 ⓪   ≠a (Correspondence (Commercial))

                 Software
710 2   ≠a Muse (Sofware), Inc.

              [type of computer]
753   ≠a (Computer).

4.3.2. (19 errors)

      1_
100 (01)   ≠a Conrad, John R.

      10   [computer file]
245 (00)   ≠a Spelling bee games ≠h ([machine-readable data file]).

                Agoura Hills, Calif.
260   ≠a (California) : ≠b Edu-Ware Services, ≠c 1981.

	4 program files on : ≠b ;
300	≠a ⟨_____⟩1 computer disk ⟨; ___⟩sd., col. ⟨:⟩ ≠c 3 1/2 in. +
	≠e
	◯1 guide.

	≠a
440 0	⟨≠s⟩ DragonWare

	System requirements:
538	≠a ◯ Game paddles.

	Guide
500	≠a ⟨Manide⟩ written by Sandy Blumstrom.

	0
505 ◯	≠a Squadron -- Skyhook -- Puzzle -- Convoy.

	reading
520	
⟨525⟩	≠a Word and letter play for early spelling and ⟨rdng⟩ readiness skills.

	0 ≠x Orthography
650 ①	≠a English language ⟨≠y Orthograph⟩ and spelling.

	, Sandy.
700 1	
⟨710 10⟩	≠a Blumstrom⟨(Sandy)⟩

710 2	≠a Edu-Ware Services (Firm)

	[Atari should have a separate 753 field.]
753	≠a Apple II ⟨, Atari⟩

753	≠a Atari

4.3.3. (29 errors)

	abdomen *[blank]* multimedia
245 00	≠a Shotgun wounds to the ⟨abdominal⟩ ⟨:⟩≠h [interactive ⟨media⟩] /
	≠c produced by HumRRO, Human Resources Research Organization, in
	conjunction with Media Exchange.

	P
246 10	
⟨245 10⟩	≠a ⟨The p⟩atient in shock.

	Version
250	
⟨251⟩	≠a ⟨Verson⟩ 2.0

256	≠a Computer data and program.

        [blank]   :   ,
260 ⓪   ≠a San Diego, Calif. ⟨;⟩ ≠b Intelligent Images ⟨;⟩ ≠c c1984.

                ≠b   ≠c   in.
300   ≠a 1 videodisc : ⟨◯⟩ sd., col. with b&w ; ⟨≠s⟩ 12 ⟨cm.⟩

300
⟨301⟩   ≠a 1 computer disk ; ≠c 5 1/4 in.

300
⟨302⟩   ≠a 1 guide.

      0_   ≠v
490 ⟨◯⟩   ≠a Dxter. Emergency/critical care ; ⟨≠p⟩ 1010061

    538   System requirements for v
⟨500⟩   ≠a ⟨   V⟩ideodisc: Pioneer or Sony videodisc player.

    538   System requirements for c
⟨500⟩   ≠a ⟨   C⟩omputer disk: IBM XT or higher; 640K; IBM InfoWindow system or compatible.

                 label
500   ≠a Title from videodisc ⟨lable⟩ .

    500   *[delete]*
⟨501⟩   ≠a Variant title on guide: The ⟨the⟩ patient in shock.

    500   ≠a   disk
⟨502⟩   ⟨◯⟩ "CD-ROM contains text data base and floppy ⟨disc⟩ contains the installation/retrieval software"--package.

508
⟨511⟩   ≠a Credits: David Allan, Gail Walaven; William C. Shoemaker.

       _0
650 ⟨◯⟩   ≠a Gunshot wounds.

4.3.4. (16 errors)

        ≠a   ≠h   / ≠c
245 00   ⟨≠t⟩ Interactive technology sampler ⟨≠a⟩ [videorecording] ⟨≠C⟩ from the National Library of Medicine.

              Computer program
256   ≠a ⟨Program⟩ .

               Md.   ≠b The Library   ≠c
260   ≠a Bethesda, ⟨MD.⟩ : ⟨The National Library⟩ , ⟨≠a⟩ 1990.

300   ≠a 1 videodisc : ≠b (col., sd.) ; ≠c 12 in. ◯ ≠e 1 leaflet.

(above: sd., col.) *(above right: +)*

538   ≠a System (rqmts.): Sony Pioneer models 6000 or 8000 with keypad for Level II or Laser Barcode compatible player with barcode wand.

(above: requirements)

500
(510)   ≠a Subtitle on leaflet: A videodisc of applications in (ehalth) care.

(above: health)

500   ≠a Issued also as interactive media with separate computer disks for IBM or Macintosh versions.

508   ≠a Producers: Craig Locatis ... [(and others)].

(above: et al.)

700   Locatis, Craig
(710) 1   ≠a (Craig Locatis).

      2
710 (1)   ≠a National Library of Medicine (U.S.)

4.3.5. (12 errors)

245 00
(240 10)   ≠a Laboratory medicine video library ≠h [videorecording] : ≠b atlas of hematology / ≠c a collaborative effort of the University of Washington departments and facilities and the Health Science Videodisc Development Group.

260   Wash.   ≠c
(256)   ≠a [Seattle, (Wash., D.C.)] : ≠b The University, (≠y) 1985.

300   ≠a 1 videodisc : ≠b (silent), col. ; ≠c 12 in. + ◯1 guide.

(above: si.) *(above right: ≠e)*

508   ≠a Editor/producer, James Fine ; principal (microscopes), Yvonne Betson, Marilyn Ostertag.

(above: microscopists)

     _0   ≠a
650 (0)   (≠s) Pharmacopeia (≠x Computer programs.)

     1_   Fine, James
700 (10)   ≠a (James, Fine).

4.3.6. (10 errors)

```
            04                              computer file
245 (14)    ≠a The reality of youth ≠h [(machine-readable data file)] / ≠c conducted by
            Robert B. Sharp, Inc.

            10
246 (14)    ≠a 501 survey of youth.

250
(256)       ≠a Version 9.155

                                           records
256         ≠a Computer data (2 files : 1457, 2797 (recordings) ).

260
(261)       ≠a Albuquerque, N.M. : ≠b 501 Inc., ≠c 1997.

500         ≠a Title from codebook.

                          survey
500         ≠a Also called 501 (servay) of youth.

500         Documentation
(501)       ≠a (Documented) written by: Rob Sharp and Carol B. Sharp.

538         ≠a Mode of access: Mainframe computer in a time-sharing environment.

700 1_
(650 10)    ≠a Sharp, Robert B.
```

4.3.7. (7 errors)

```
            Storm   ≠h  [interactive multimedia]
245 00      ≠a Desert (Strom) (≠a) ([Interactive Multimedia]) : ≠b the war in the Persian
            Gulf / ≠c Warner New Media in association with Time Magazine.

260         ≠a Burbank, CA : ≠b Warner New Media, ≠c 1991.

                               ≠b              ≠c 4 3/4
300         ≠a 1 computer optical disc : ( ) sd., col. ; ( )(5) in.

538
(548)       ≠a System requirements: Macintosh Plus or newer; at least 1M RAM (color
            machines require 2M RAM); System 6.0.5 or later; Apple-compatible SCSI
            CD-ROM drive.

500         ≠a Title from title screens.

650  0      ≠a Persian Gulf War, 1991.
```

4.3.8. (1 error)

	Kans.
260	≠a Selina, (Kansas) : ≠b Sewell Music Co., ≠c c1996.

4.4. Computer Files, 008 (Header) Information Exercise Answers

4.4.1.   Target audience

a.   __b__

b.   __b__

c.   __d__

d.   __e__

e.   __g__

4.4.2.   Type of computer file

a.   __i__

b.   __g__

c.   __a__

d.   __d__

e.   __f__

f.   __j__

g.   __z__

h.   __b__

4.4.3.   Government publication

a.   __c__

b.   __s__

c.   __f__

d.   __m__

e.   __a__

f.   __l__

g.   ____

4.4.4.   008 . . . . . . s1984 . . . . mou . . . g . . . b . . . . eng . d

4.4.5.   008 . . . . . . s1984 . . . . miu . . . g . . . b . . . . eng . d

4.4.6.   008 . . . . . . s1984 . . . . miu . . . g . . . b . . . . eng . d

4.4.7.   008 . . . . . . s1984 . . . . lau . . . g . . . c . . . . eng . d

4.4.8.   008 . . . . . . s1984 . . . . lau . . . g . . . b . . . . eng . d

4.4.9.   008 . . . . . . m19899999lau . . . g . . . j . s . . . . . eng . d

4.4.10. 008 . . . . . . m19919999lau . . . . e . . . j . s . . . . . eng . d

4.4.11. 008 . . . . . . m19909999nyu . . . . e . . . j . s . . . . . eng . d

4.5. Computer Files, *AACR2R* Chapter 9 Exercise Answers

4.5.1.   Description of files that are encoded for manipulation by computer, both data and programs. Materials may be stored on, or contained in, carriers available for direct access or by remote access.

4.5.2.   Electronic devices such as calculators, etc.

4.5.3.   When it is the only name given in the chief source.

4.5.4.   Information showing that this issue contains differences from other editions of that file, or to a named reissue of a file. Some examples might be preliminary releases, versions or updates, differing levels or releases, or software usable on different makes of computers (Apple vs. IBM).

4.5.5.   In case of doubt, don't. You may put in a note if you so desire.

4.5.6.   Computer cartridge, computer cassette, computer disk, computer reel.

4.5.7.   Give the specific name of the physical carrier as concisely as possible, preferably qualified by "computer", as in "1 computer card".

4.5.8.   *AACR2R* rule 1.5E. Rule 9.5E1 tells you this.

4.5.9.   The title screen(s) or, in the absence of such, other internal evidence (main menus, program statements).

4.5.10. The physical carrier or its labels, information issued by the publisher with the file (documentation), or information printed on the container issued by the publisher, distributor, etc.

4.5.11. Use "Multimedia" or "Kit", as instructed in rules 1.1C1 and 1.10C1.

4.5.12. Put the source of the edition statement in a separate note.

4.5.13. Computer data, Computer program(s), Computer data and program(s).

4.5.14. Only when the sound is an integral part of the software, not just beeps or bongs.

4.5.15. Rule 9.7B says to give a particular note first when it has been decided that that note is of primary importance.

4.5.16. Use the source with the unifying element as the chief source if it gives a collective title and the most complete information, and the parts themselves do not.

4.5.17. Yes, include a GMD for all nonprint materials.

4.5.18. *Edition, issue, version, release, level, update,* or their equivalents in other languages.

4.5.19. Record the file characteristics with type of file (data, program, or both), number of records, statements, etc., and inclusive lengths.

4.5.20. Omit it from the bibliographic record.

4.5.21. Disks are given in inches, to the next ¼ inch up; cartridges are given in inches for the length of the side of the cartridge that is to be inserted into the machine.

4.5.22. Nature and scope and system requirements (including mode of access); Language and script; Source of title proper; Variations in title; Parallel titles and other title information; Statements of responsibility; Edition and history; File characteristics; Publication, distribution, etc.; Physical description; Accompanying material; Series; Dissertations; Audience; Other formats; Summary; Contents; Numbers; Copy being described, library's holdings, and restrictions on use; "With" notes.

4.5.23.   Yes.

4.5.24.   The persons or bodies responsible for the content of the file.

4.5.25.   No.

4.5.26.   Record only the date of creation.

4.5.27.   Computer reels.

4.5.28.   Yes, as instructed in rule 1.8E.

5.1. Maps, Full Records Tagging Exercise Answers

5.1.1.   110 1   ≠a Louisiana. ≠b Dept. of Transportation and Development. ≠c Traffic and Planning Division.

         245 1 0   ≠a Map of Louisiana showing state-maintained highway system ≠h [map].

         246 1 0   ≠a Louisiana highway system.

         255   ≠a Scales vary.

         260   ≠a [Baton Rouge] : ≠b The Division, ≠c 1992.

         300   ≠a 92 maps : ≠b b&w ; ≠c 44 × 49 cm. on sheets 47 × 63 cm.

         500   ≠a Some maps include index and/or location insert.

         500   ≠a Also includes 1992 Louisiana railway system, official control section maps for districts, and detailed maps of each parish.

5.1.2.   110 2 0   ≠a Committee for the Preservation of the Port Hudson Battlefield.

         245 1 2   ≠a A collection of maps for those persons interested in Port Hudson Battlefield ≠h [map].

         246 1 0   ≠a Port Hudson Battlefield.

         255   ≠a Scales vary.

         260   ≠a [Baton Rouge, La.] : ≠b The Committee, ≠c c1964.

         300   ≠a 14 maps : ≠b some col. ; ≠c 58 × 45 cm. - 72 × 90 cm. + ≠e 1 text (5 leaves).

         500   ≠a Title from cover of portfolio.

5.1.3.   110 1   ≠a Louisiana. ≠b Dept. of Public Works.

         245 1 0   ≠a [Old levee drawings concerning Port Allen and W.B.R. Parish] ≠h [map].

         246 1 0   ≠a Port Allen levees.

         246 1 0   ≠a West Baton Rouge Parish levees.

         255   ≠a Scales vary.

         260   ≠a [Port Allen, La.] : ≠b R.D. Landry, ≠c 1976.

         300   ≠a 10 maps : ≠b b&w ; ≠c 40 × 50 cm. on sheets 45 × 64 cm. + ≠e 2 sheets of explanatory notes.

         500   ≠a Title supplied by cataloger taken from attached in-house label.

         500   ≠a Photoprint from microfilm.

5.1.4.   110 1   ≠a West Baton Rouge Parish (La.). ≠b Assessor's Office.

         245 1 0   ≠a West Baton Rouge Parish ≠h [map] : ≠b index to rural maps.

246	1 0	≠a Index to rural maps.
255		≠a Scales vary.
260		≠a [Port Allen, La. : ≠b The Office, ≠c 198-?]
300		≠a 1 map : ≠b photocopy ; ≠c 73 × 96 cm. on sheet 76 × 106 cm.
500		≠a Blue line print.
500		≠a With enlargements of Wards 2, 3, and 4.

5.1.5.

110	2	≠a Ashburn Maps.
245	1 0	≠a City map of Alexandria and Pineville ≠h [map] / ≠c Ashburn Maps ; compliments of Stephens Agency, Inc.
255		≠a Scale [ca. 1:23344] ; ≠a 1:380160.
260		≠a Fort Worth, Tex. : ≠b Ashburn Maps, ≠a 1971.
300		≠a 1 map : ≠b col. ; ≠c 58 × 43 cm., folded to 23 × 11 cm.
500		≠a Scale is given as 1 1/4 inch to 1/2 mile.
500		≠a Includes street indexes.
500		≠a Panel title.
500		≠a Includes inset map of England Air Force Base.
500		≠a Includes ancillary maps of Rapides Parish, Pineville Central Business District and Alexandria Central Business District.
651	0	≠a Alexandria (La.) ≠x Maps.
651	0	≠a Pineville (La.) ≠x Maps.
651	0	≠a Rapides Parish (La.) ≠x Maps.

5.1.6.

100	1	≠a Crawford, Andrew, ≠c Surveyor.
245	1 0	≠a Plan of the United States public grounds, Baton Rouge, La. ≠h [map] / ≠c A. Crawford, surveyor.
255		≠a Scale 1:4800.
260		≠a [S.l. : ≠b s.n.], ≠c 1839.
300		≠a 1 map ; ≠c 45 × 61 cm.
500		≠a References list the number of acres of swamp, woodland, etc., and the number of acres in lots such as hospital lot and ordnance lot.
500		≠a Magnetic variation 8°45' E. on recto.
500		≠a Selected buildings and trees shown pictorially.
500		≠a "C-109-2"
651	0	≠a Baton Rouge (La.) ≠x Maps.

5.1.7.

100	1	≠a United States. ≠b Commodity Stabilization Service.
245	1 0	≠a E. Baton Rouge Parish, Louisiana ≠h [map] / ≠c U.S. Department of Agriculture, Commodity Stabilization Service.
255		≠a Scale 1:20,000.
260		≠a [Washington, D.C.] : ≠b The Service, ≠c 1959.
300		≠a 1 remote-sensing image ; ≠c 47 × 45 cm.
500		≠a Imaging produced by Coloramic Aerial Surveys Corp., subcontractor, Woltz Studios, Inc., Des Moines, IA.

650   0 ≠a East Baton Rouge Parish (La.) ≠x Maps.

650   0 ≠a Aerial photographs.

710 2 ≠a Coloramic Aerial Surveys Corp.

710 2 ≠a Woltz Studios.

5.1.8.   245 0 0 ≠a Plan of Fort Baton Rouge ≠h [map].

255   ≠a Scale [ca. 1:6,480].

260   ≠a [S.l. : ≠b s.n., ≠c 1800?]

300   ≠a 1 map : ≠b photocopy ; ≠c 31 × 54 cm.

500   ≠a In: Collot, Georges Henri Victor. A journey in North America ... 1924. pl. #35.

500   ≠a Oriented with north to the left.

500   ≠a Scale is given in fathoms; 1 fathom equals 6 feet.

500   ≠a Fort, selected buildings and trees shown pictorially.

500   ≠a Relief shown by shading.

651   0 ≠a Fort Baton Rouge (La.) ≠x Maps.

651   0 ≠a Baton Rouge (La.) ≠x Maps.

5.2. Maps, Notes Exercise Answers

Plan of the lots reserved for Spanish families of Galvez Town

8
10
5
2
9
4
6
3
1
7

5.3. Maps, Error Identification Exercise Answers

5.3.1. (10 errors)

110 2

(100 1) ≠a Miller, Smith, & Champagne, Inc.

10   ≠h

245 (20) ≠a West Baton Rouge Parish roads ( ) [map].

Scale
255   ≠a ⟨⎯⎯⎯⟩ 1:63,360.

[blank]   ≠b   Miller, Smith, & Champagne,
260 ⓪   ≠a [Baton Rouge, La.] : ⟨≠B⟩ ⟨Miller, Champagne, and Smith],⟩ ≠c 1992.

                                               [blank]
300   ≠a 1 map : ≠b photocopy ; ≠c 71 × 51 cm. ⟨≠c⟩ on sheet 107 × 77 cm.

500
⟨505⟩   ≠a Blue line print.

500   ≠a Includes location insets.

651 _0
⟨650 0⟩ ≠a West Baton Rouge Parish (La.) ≠x Road maps.

5.3.2. (17 errors)

100   ≠d
⟨110⟩ 1 ≠a Albert, Gerald, ⟨≠c⟩ 1917-

      1 0   [map]
245 ⟨1 4⟩ ≠a Road closings in Richmond County, October 1977 ≠h ⟨[maps]⟩.

[blank]   [blank] 1:63,300
255 ⟨2⟩   ≠a Scale ⟨:⟩ ⟨1-63300⟩ .

300   :   ≠c
⟨301⟩   ≠a 1 map ⟨;⟩ ≠b col. ; ⟨≠a⟩ 28 cm.

      0
440 ⟨4⟩   ≠a Road closures, Richmond County

          Oriented
500   ≠a ⟨Orinted⟩ with north to top left.

500   to be
⟨504⟩   ≠a Intended ⟨tobe⟩ given out to the public.

      _ 0   (Va.)   ≠x
651⟨0⟩   ≠a Richmond County ⟨, Virginia⟩ ⟨≠z⟩ Road maps.

5.3.3. (25 errors)

110   (U.S.)
⟨100⟩ 2 ≠a Geological Survey ⟨(U.S.A.)⟩

                1 0   [map]
245 (1 4)   ≠a Miami quadrangle, Florida--Dade Co., 1988 ≠h (map) : ≠b 7.5 minute
                    (topographic)
            series ((topogrphic)) / ≠c mapped, edited and published by the Geological
            Survey.

       [blank]   1:24,000
255 (2)   ≠a Scale (1-24,000) ; ≠b transverse Mercator proj.
                  (W 80°15'00"--W 80°07'30"/N 25°52'30"--N 25°45'00").
          ≠c (w80°15'00" ; w80°07'30" by n25°52'30" ; n25°45'00")

          ≠a   Va.   Colo.
260   (≠b) Reston, (Virginia) : ≠b The Survey ; ≠a Denver, (Colorado) : For sale by the
            Survey, ≠c [1992].

300   :   ≠c
(301)   ≠a 1 map (;) ≠b col. ; (≠a) 28 cm.

500 [blank]   and   .
(504)(4)   ≠a Relief shown by contours (,) spot heights (, and contours.)

                 Depths
500   ≠a (Deaths) shown by isolines and soundings.

500
(504)   ≠a "Map photoinspected 1990; no major culture or drainage observed."--Map
            verso.

          ≠a
500   ( ) Includes quadrangle location map.

                          [blank]
500   ≠a "DMA 4935 I SW ; (≠v) Series V847"

       _ 0   ≠x   Topographic
651 (0)   ≠a Florida (≠z) Maps, (topographic).

5.3.4. (13 errors)

      110
(220) 2   ≠a Satellite Snaps, Inc.

                1 0   ≠h [map]
245 (0 0)   ≠a Fort Lauderdale from LANDSAT 5 ( ) / ≠c this print produced and
            distributed by Satellite Snaps, Inc. ; image enhancement by KRS Remote
            Sensing ; Landsat data distributed by the Earth Observation Satellite Company.

      255
(256)   ≠a Scale not given.

	Md.]	
260	≠a [Ridgely, (Maryland) ( ) : ≠b Satellite Snaps, ≠c c1999.	

[delete sd.]

300 ≠a 1 remote sensing image : ≠b (sd.,) col. ; ≠c 90 × 46 cm.

500
(300) ≠a Landsat remote sensing image, processed to simulate natural color.

≠a
500 ( ) Shows Fort Lauderdale metropolitan area.

590
(589) ≠a Library's copy encapsulated in plastic.

Florida ≠z Fort Lauderdale Region.
650 0 ≠a Remote sensing ≠z (Fort Lauderdale Region, Florida.)

651   Photo maps
(650) 0 ≠a Fort Lauderdale Region (Fla.) ≠x (Photographic maps) .

5.3.5. (18 errors)

1   ≠b
110 ( ) ≠a Morocco. (≠B) Idarat al-Maadin wa-al-Jiyulujiyah.

=
245 1 0 ≠a Carte tectonique internationale de l'Afrique ( ) ≠b International tectonic
/
map of Africa ( ) ≠c compiled by the Geological Survey of Morocco.

260 ≠a [Paris] : ≠b Association of African Geological Surveys, ≠c c1969.

300   1 map : ≠b col.   cm.
(301) ≠a (col. map   ) ; ≠c 182 × 182 cm. on 9 sheets 68 × 98 - 68 × 93 (centimeters.)

_ 0   ≠v v.4
440 (0) ≠a Earth sciences ; (≠v4)

255   .
(507) ≠a Scale 1:5,000,000 ( )

500
(600) ≠a Depths shown by contours and soundings.

500   index
(504) ≠a Includes (indx) map and inset.

1964
500 ≠a Shows tectonics information as of (1694) .

650   ≠z   ≠x

(651) 0   ≠a Geology (≠x) Africa (≠z) Maps.

5.3.6. (10 errors)

100 1

(110 2 0) ≠a Kneeland, Ira C.

245 1 0

(240 1 1) ≠a [Baton Rouge] ≠h [map] / ≠c Ira C. Kneeland, surveyor.

           ≠a

255   ◯ Scale not given.

        [S.l. : ≠b s.n.]   ,

260   ≠a ([S.l.] : ≠b [s.n.]) (;) ≠c 1809.

                photocopy   ;

300   ≠a 1 map : ≠b (Xerox copy) (:) ≠c 54 × 38 cm.

500   ≠a Title supplied by cataloger.

           ≠a

500   (≠y) "1809" handwritten in lower left hand corner.

500

(560)   ≠a Shows four public lots for the use of the church, etc.

651   0

(655   7) ≠a Baton Rouge (La.) ≠x Maps.

5.3.7. (1 error)

245

(246) 1 0   ≠a Miami to Marathon and Florida Bay, Florida ≠h [map] / ≠c National
Ocean Service.

5.3.8. (23 errors)

110   Ordnance

(120) 1   ≠a Great Britain. ≠b (Ordinance) Survey.

     1 0   Cayman   made

245 (1 4) ≠a (Caman) Islands, visitors map ≠h [map] / ≠c (nade) and published by the
                Survey   assistance
Ordnance (Survay), Southampton, England with the (asstance) of the
Cayman Islands Government.

255   ≠a Scale 1:50,000 ⟨≠a⟩ (W 81°25'-- W 79°45'/N 19°45'--N 19°15').
⤷ ≠c

260   ⟨≠x⟩ ⟨Southhampton⟩ : ≠b The ⟨Survay⟩ ; ≠a Grand ⟨Caman⟩ , Cayman Islands : ≠b Dept. of Tourism, ≠c 1989.
⤷ ≠a Southampton   ⤷ Survey   ⤷ Cayman

300   ≠a 3 maps on 1 sheet : ≠b col. ; ≠a 36 × 76 ⟨in.⟩ or smaller, sheet 79 by 99 ⟨in.⟩, folded to 20 × 13 ⟨in.⟩
⤷ cm.   ⤷ cm.   ⤷ cm.

⟨504⟩   ≠a Panel ⟨titel⟩ .
⤷ 500   ⤷ title

⟨520⟩   ≠a Includes text, location map, and ancillary maps of "Air communications" and "George Town."
⤷ 500

505 ⟨3⟩   ≠a Grand Cayman -- Little ⟨Caman⟩ -- ⟨Caiman⟩ Brac.
⤷ 0   ⤷ Cayman   ⤷ Cayman

651   0   ≠a ⟨Caiman⟩ Islands ≠x ⟨Tourist maps⟩ .
⤷ Cayman   ⤷ Maps, Tourist

5.4. Maps, 008 (Header) Information Exercise Answers

5.4.1.   Relief information

a.   k
b.   e
c.   g
d.   a
e.   d
f.   c
g.   ___
h.   z

5.4.2.   Projection

a.   bd
b.   be
c.   ae
d.   ag
e.   bj
f.   da

    g.   <u>db</u>

    h.   <u>bs</u>

    i.   <u>dg</u>

    j.   <u>cb</u>

    k.   <u>zz</u>

5.4.3. Type of cartographic matter

    a.   <u>d</u>

    b.   <u>b</u>

    c.   <u>e</u>

    d.   <u>a</u>

    e.   <u>c</u>

5.4.4. Government publications

    a.   <u>l</u>

    b.   <u>f</u>

    c.   <u>s</u>

    d.   <u>i</u>

    e.   <u>   </u>

    f.   <u>c</u>

    g.   <u>m</u>

5.4.5. Special format characteristics

    a.   <u>o</u>

    b.   <u>k</u>

    c.   <u>l</u>

    d.   <u>m</u>

    e.   <u>j</u>

    f.   <u>q</u>

    g.   <u>r</u>

    h.   <u>e</u>

5.4.6. 008 . . . . . . s1960 . . . . nyui . . . . a . . . . . 0 . . . eng . d

5.4.7. 008 . . . . . . s1931 . . . . nyu . . . . a . f . . 0 . . . eng . d

5.4.8. 008 . . . . . . s1879 . . . . dcu . . . . a . f . . 0 . . . eng . d

5.4.9. 008 . . . . . . s1921 . . . . nyu . . . . a . . . . . 0 . . . eng . d

5.4.10. 008 . . . . . . s1799 . . . . xxu . . . . a . . . . . 0 . . . eng . d

5.4.11. 008 . . . . . . s1938 . . . . xxui . . . . . a . . . . . 1 . . . eng . d

5.4.12. 008 . . . . . . s1990 . . . . lau . . . . a . . . . . 1 . . . eng . d

5.4.13. 008 . . . . . . s1992 . . . . lau . . . . a . . . . . 1 . . . eng . d

5.5. Maps, *AACR2R* Chapter 3 Exercise Answers

5.5.1. All materials that represent the whole or part of the earth or any celestial body. These include two- and three-dimensional maps and plans (including imaginary places); aeronautical, navigational, and celestial charts; atlases; globes; block diagrams; sections; aerial photographs; bird's-eye views, etc.

5.5.2. Description of early or manuscript cartographic materials.

5.5.3. Always include the name of the place in the supplied title.

5.5.4. Either describe the item as a collection or create individual bibliographic records for each part.

5.5.5. Create the representative fraction and put it in square brackets.

5.5.6. A note giving the scale as it appears on the item.

5.5.7. Give the vertical scale (specified as such) after the horizontal scale, if the vertical scale can be determined.

5.5.8. The straight line separating the data from the border.

5.5.9. Describe it as 1 atlas, with pagination given in parentheses.

5.5.10. Give height × width in centimeters, rounding up to the nearest whole centimeter, within the neat line.

5.5.11. The item itself.

5.5.12. The container or case, the cradle and stand of a globe, etc.

5.5.13. Map ; or, Globe.

5.5.14. Create a collective title and put it in square brackets.

5.5.15. Compute a representative fraction from a bar graph or a grid, or compare it to a map whose scale is known. Give the information in square brackets preceded by "ca."

5.5.16. In the 255 field put "Scale indeterminable."

5.5.17. When it is found on the item.

5.5.18. Add "braille", "tactile", "Press braille", or "solid dot braille" to the extent of item, in parentheses.

5.5.19. Nature and scope of the item; Language; Source of title proper; Variations in title; Parallel titles and other title information; Statements of responsibility; Edition and history; Mathematical and other cartographic data; Publication, distribution, etc.; Physical description; Accompanying material; Series; Dissertations; Audience; Other formats; Contents; Numbers; Copy described, library's holdings, and restrictions on use; and "With" notes.

5.5.20. The front, or side intended to be used first.

5.5.21. Either as a whole or describe each map separately, giving the name of the collection as a series.

5.5.22. Use the designation for the predominant part. If neither is predominant, use either **multimedia** or **kit**.

5.5.23. No; the scale field always contains English words and abbreviations.

5.5.24. Give both scales connected with a hyphen, smaller scale first.

5.5.25. In the 255 field put "Scales vary."

5.5.26. Atlas, diagram, globe, map, map section, profile, relief model, remote-sensing image, view.

5.5.27.　Use a specific term taken from rule X.5B in one of the chapters in part I; for example, 7 wall charts or 52 playing cards.

5.5.28.　Number of maps in an atlas, color, material, mounting.

5.5.29.　When it is stated in the item.

5.5.30.　Yes.

5.5.31.　Supply one, with a note about the source of the title. Put the title in square brackets.

5.5.32.　Add the location in square brackets as a subtitle.

5.5.33.　As a representative fraction expressed as a ratio (1:).

5.5.34.　Give a statement of scale only if the information appears on the item. If it is not drawn to scale, in the 255 field put "Not drawn to scale".

5.5.35.　Give the number of sheets and the number of segments; for example, 1 map section in 6 segments or 1 map on 6 sheets.

5.5.36.　Give the material on which it is printed if it is considered significant; for example, plastic, silk, wood, or vellum.

6.1. Kits, Full Records Tagging Exercise Answers

6.1.1.　245 0 0　≠a Kinderkit ≠h [kit] : ≠b kindergarten.

　　　　260　　　≠a LaSalle, Ill. : ≠b Open Court, ≠c c1989.

　　　　300　　　≠a 1 set activity sheets, 2 sets of masters, 1 brown bear puppet, 1 record, 1 booklet, 1 cassette, 1 set of picture cards, 2 books, 1 set of wall cards, 1 set individual cards (4 copies), 1 set of flash cards (4 copies), 1 picture pack, 1 set of color cards, 1 set of shape cards.

　　　　440　0　≠a Open Court reading and writing

　　　　500　　　≠a Designed to be used with First star readiness teacher's guide in the Open Court reading and writing program.

　　　　520　　　≠a Teaches the alphabet in introducing the student to reading.

　　　　650　0　≠a Reading (Primary)

　　　　650　0　≠a Alphabet ≠x Study and teaching (Primary)

　　　　650　0　≠a English language ≠x Alphabet ≠x Study and teaching (Primary)

6.1.2.　245 0 0　≠a Environments ≠h [kit].

　　　　260　　　≠a New York : ≠b Scholastic, ≠c 1991.

　　　　300　　　≠a 1 sound cassette, 9 song charts, 1 paperback book (6 copies), 1 teaching plan, 1 banner.

　　　　440　0　≠a Scholastic banners

　　　　500　　　≠a Paperback book is entitled Earth songs, by Myra Cohn Livingston, poet, and Leonard Everett Fisher, painter.

　　　　500　　　≠a Sound cassette contains songs focusing on environmental concerns and interests.

　　　　520　　　≠a Uses a variety of materials to develop a program focusing on the environment.

	650	0	≠a Habitat (Ecology)
	650	0	≠a Ecology.
	700	1	≠a Livingston, Myra Cohn. ≠t Earth songs.

6.1.3.   245 0 0   ≠a SCREEN ≠h [kit] : ≠b screening children for related early educational needs / ≠c Wayne P. Hresko ... [et al.].

246 3 0   ≠a Screening children for related early educational needs.

260   ≠a Austin, Tex. : ≠b Pro-Ed, ≠c c1988.

300   ≠a 1 profile/record form (25 copies), 1 student workbook (25 copies), 1 picture book, l examiner's manual, in container 17 × 26 × 3 cm.

508   ≠a Developed by Wayne P. Hresko, D. Kim Reid, Donald D. Hammill, Herbert P. Ginsburg, Arthur J. Baroody.

520   ≠a A measure of early academic proficiencies in the areas of oral language, reading, writing, and mathematics. Standardized research tool for early childhood programs that complies with standards of the American Psychological Association. For children ages 3-7. Useful for identifying mildly handicapped students.

650   0   ≠a Mentally handicapped children ≠x Ability testing.

650   0   ≠a Learning ability ≠x Testing.

650   0   ≠a Early Learning Skills Analysis.

650   0   ≠a Early children education ≠x Activity programs.

650   0   ≠a Educational tests and measurements.

650   0   ≠a Preschool children ≠x Ability testing.

700   1   ≠a Hresko, Wayne P.

6.1.4.   245 0 0   ≠a Algebra ≠h [kit].

260   ≠a Glenview, Ill. : ≠b Scott Foresman, ≠c c1996.

300   ≠a 1 activity sourcebook, 1 geometry template, 8 overhead transparencies, 1 clear vinyl case (24 × 31 cm.)

500   ≠a "University of Chicago School Mathematics Project."

500   ≠a "The Activity Sourcebook is a collection of activities in blackline-master form accompanied by Teacher's notes designed to provide options in the teaching of lessons in UCSMP Algebra. The Activity kit includes eight overhead transparencies that aid in classroom discussion of the activities."--Introduction.

650   0   ≠a Algebra ≠x Study and teaching.

710   2   ≠a University of Chicago. ≠b School Mathematics Project.

6.1.5.   100   1   ≠a Erickson, Lynn Martin.

245 0 0   ≠a Remembering birthdays ≠h [kit] / ≠c by Lynn Martin Erickson and Kathryn Leide.

260   ≠a Madison, Wisc. : ≠b Bi-Folkal Productions, ≠c 1982.

300		≠a 1 videocassette, 1 sound cassette, 1 program manual (2 copies), 1 booklet (Happy birthday), 1 booklet (Many happy returns) (25 copies), 2 graphics masters, 4 skit scripts (3 copies of each), 1 booklet (According to astrology) (25 copies) and 1 bag containing cake decorating tips, 2 candle holders, and an introduction to antique birthday cards, in canvas carryall.
500		≠a Title from data sheet.
520		≠a Designed to assist program leaders who work with groups of mentally alert older people in evoking memories of birthdays.
650	0	≠a Birthdays.
700	1	≠a Leide, Kathryn.

6.1.6.

245	0 0	≠a Reminiscing ≠h [kit] : ≠b the game for people over thirty.
260		≠a Glendale Heights, IL : ≠b TDC Games, ≠c 1989.
300		≠a 1 game (17 pieces), 1 game/score board, 1 reminiscing booklet, 3 dice, 4 decade booklets, 8 pawns, in container 46 × 19 × 8 cm.
500		≠a For 2 to 4 players or teams.
521		≠a Intended audience: persons over thirty years of age.
520		≠a Takes you through the years 1939-1979.
650	0	≠a Memories.
655	7	≠a Games. ≠2 lcsh

6.1.7.

245	0 0	≠a Mathematics ≠h [kit] : ≠b exploring your world.
260		≠a Morristown, N.J. : ≠b Silver Burdett & Ginn, ≠c c1995.
300		≠a 9 kits containing overhead transparencies, manipulative connection cards, test booklets, home school connection booklets, and teacher editions of Applying my skills booklets, authentic assessment booklets, chapter support materials files, answer key booklets.
500		≠a 7 kits (grades K, 1, 2, 3, 4, 6, 7) in tote bags 34 × 36 × 12 cm. ; 2 kits (grades 5, 8) in tote bags 64 × 56 × 9 cm.
500		≠a Kits for Grades K-2 do not contain overhead transparencies.
650	0	≠a Mathematics ≠x Study and teaching (Elementary)
650	0	≠a Arithmetic ≠x Study and teaching (Elementary)

6.1.8.

245	0 0	≠a [Game pieces] ≠h [kit].
260		≠a [Atlanta, Ga. : ≠b Play Rugs Corp., ≠c 1967].
300		≠a 2 rings, 1 pole, 24 checkers (12 red, 12 black), 60 marbles (10 each red, orange, blue, green, purple, black), 4 horseshoes (plastic), 2 poles, 32 chess pieces (16 black, 16 red) in box 28 × 28 × 22 cm.
500		≠a Title supplied by cataloger.
520		≠a Designed to be used with game boards printed into a rug to be used in a recreation room.
650	0	≠a Games.
650	0	≠a Board games.

6.2. Kits, Error Identification Exercise Answers

6.2.1. (18 errors)

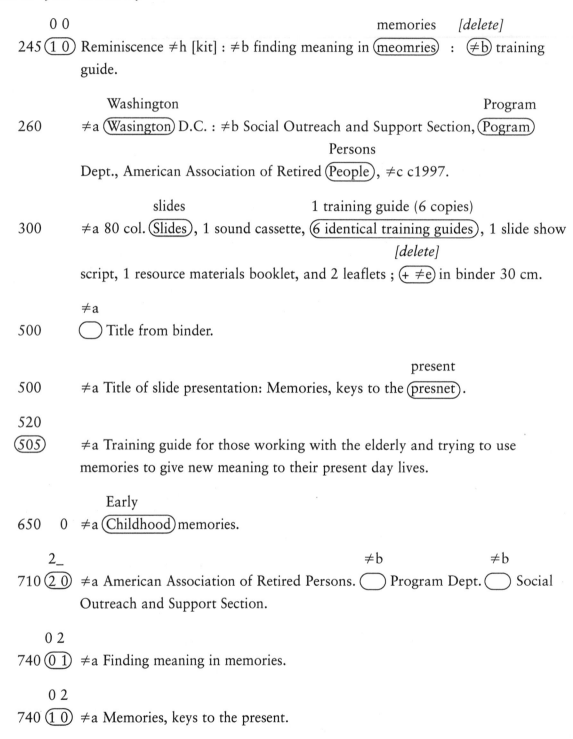

         0 0   memories   *[delete]*

245 (1 0) Reminiscence ≠h [kit] : ≠b finding meaning in (meomries) : (≠b) training guide.

               Washington   Program

260   ≠a (Wasington) D.C. : ≠b Social Outreach and Support Section, (Pogram)

                                       Persons

Dept., American Association of Retired (People), ≠c c1997.

                  slides   1 training guide (6 copies)

300   ≠a 80 col. (Slides), 1 sound cassette, (6 identical training guides), 1 slide show

                                           [delete]

script, 1 resource materials booklet, and 2 leaflets ; (+ ≠e) in binder 30 cm.

          ≠a

500   ( ) Title from binder.

                                                    present

500   ≠a Title of slide presentation: Memories, keys to the (presnet).

520

(505)   ≠a Training guide for those working with the elderly and trying to use memories to give new meaning to their present day lives.

               Early

650   0   ≠a (Childhood) memories.

        2_   ≠b   ≠b

710 (2 0) ≠a American Association of Retired Persons. ( ) Program Dept. ( ) Social Outreach and Support Section.

        0 2

740 (0 1) ≠a Finding meaning in memories.

        0 2

740 (1 0) ≠a Memories, keys to the present.

6.2.2. (9 errors)

00   [kit]

245 (1 0) ≠a Mathematics ≠h (activity kit) : ≠b manipulative activity kit.

                                    ≠b

260   ≠a White Plains, NY : ◯ Cuisenaire Company of America,

         ≠c *[delete copyright symbol]*

         ◯   ©[1997?]

[replace all dashes with commas; counts as 1 error]

300   ≠a 411 color tiles ⊖600 snap cubes ⊖72 color dice ⊖12 number cubes ⊖

         15 counter bowls ⊖15 decks of playing cards ⊖2 menu posters, in container

         65 × 12 × 36 cm.

521

(500)   ≠a For grades 1-2.

500   ≠a Title from container.

                                          (Primary)

650   0 ≠a Mathematics ≠x Study and teaching ((Grades 1, 2))

         Creative activities and seatwork

650   0 ≠a (Seatwork and activities).

6.2.3. (10 errors)

700 1

(100 1) ≠a Charles, Linda.

245   ≠n

(240)0 0 ≠a Mathland ≠h [kit] : ≠b journeys through mathematics. (≠p) Grade 1 /

         ≠c

         (≠a) Linda Charles ... [et al.].

         Mountain   *[blank]*

260   ≠a (Muontain) View, CA (.): ≠b Creative Publications, ≠c c1998.

300

(505 0) ≠a 1 guidebook, 1 resource manager, 1 assessment guide, 1 daily tune-ups, 1 skill power teacher's edition, 1 videocassette, 1 calculator, assorted supplementary materials, 1 arithmetwists, 1 arithmetwists reproducibles, 1 arithmetwists teacher's edition, 1 skill power, 1 skill power reproducibles, 1 bridges to home reproducibles, assorted consumable and/or manipulative materials, in box 46 × 65 × 51 cm.

500

(520) ≠a Videocassette, A peek into Mathland, is an overview of the Mathland program, its goals and use of the components in the kit.

       Mathematics   *[blank]*

650 0 ≠a (Math) ≠x Study and teaching (Elementary) (.)

6.2.4. (15 errors)

                [blank]   [kit]

245 0 0 ≠a Remembering train rides (.) ≠h (KIT) / ≠c designed by Lynne Erickson and Kathryn Leide.

260   *[delete delimiter]*

(262) ≠a Madison : ≠b Bi-Folkal Productions, (≠b) University of Wisconsin-Madison Library School, ≠c 1977.

300 ≠a 1 Amtrak map (35 × 53 cm.), 2 cassettes, 1 engineer's hat, printed materials, program manual, 80 slides in carousel, train paraphernalia, and 1 woman's hat in container (30 × 38 × 12 cm.)

(301) ≠a (1 kit ; 30 × 38 × 12 in.)

       0

440 (1) ≠a Media kit for the elderly

500

(505 0) ≠a Cassettes: All aboard. Sing-along. Ballads -- Large-print song sheets: 500 miles. I've been workin' on the railroad. Sentimental journey (25 copies each) -- Large-print poem sheets: From a railway carriage. Travel (25 copies each) -- 8 cards of jokes -- Skit script (When is the train due?) (4 copies) -- 1 large-print newspaper -- Photocopied masters of large-print songs and poems, including the poem The vanishing depot -- Train paraphernalia: 1 Amtrak menu, 1977. 1 Super Chief menu, 1937. 1 railroad schedule. 1 Amtrak annual report. 1 grease pen.

500   ≠a "An L.S.C.A.-funded project through the Wisconsin Division for Library Services"--p. iv, program manual.

520
(500)   ≠a Provides materials to help evoke memories of train rides; designed for program leaders who work with groups of mentally alert elderly people.

650   Railroad travel
(651)   0   ≠a (Travel, Railroad).

          Railroads
650   0   ≠a (Trains) ≠x Miscellanea.

700 1 _
(700   1)   ≠a Erickson, Lynne Martin.

700 1_   Leide, Kathryn
(700   2)   ≠a (Kathryn Leide).

6.2.5. (11 errors)

    2   Juulchin Tourist Commission.
110(1)   ≠a (Mongolia. ≠b Juulchin Tourist Commission.)

    1 0   Mongolia
245 (1 4)   ≠a Learn about (Mongoliea) ≠h [kit] / ≠c Juulchin Tourist Commission.

                  :   ≠b   ,
260   ≠a Ulaanbaatar, Mongolia (.) (≠p) The Commission (.) ≠c 1998.

          ≠a
300   (≠n) 1 "ger" model, 1 videocassette, various carvings of native Mongolian animals, 1 dictionary, 1 man's hat, 1 woman's hat, 2 sound cassettes, 15 photographs, 1 children's book in native Mongolian script, in container 38 × 62 × 18 cm.

          Title
500   ≠a (Titel) from container.

500   ≠a Designed as a promotional packet to be used by travel agents in America to attract travelers to the world's most sparsely populated country.

    0   Mongolia
651 ( )   ≠a (People's Republic of Mongolia) ≠x Description and travel.

6.2.6. (1 error)

[delete delimiters a & b—this is unpublished.]

260   ≠a [S.l. : ≠b s.n.], c1991.

6.2.7. (10 errors)

           [kit]

245 0 0   ≠a Kindersay ≠h kit .

      3 _

246 0 2   ≠a Early learning development curriculum.

260   Pa.   P
262   ≠a Devon, Penns. : ≠b PRIMAK publications, ≠c c1987-1991.

300
301   ≠a 248 flash cards, 72 lesson envelopes, activities cards inside some lesson envelopes, 1 conceptual language development book, 1 auditory discrimination [sic] auditory memory book, l placement test book, numerical index to picture file, 1 box of interactive materials, 7 envelopes of paper shapes, 2 charts, in container 26 × 32 × 25 cm.

         ≠a

500   ≠x Title from container.

         ≠a

500   Each envelope of paper shapes contains a different color: red, purple, orange, green, blue, yellow and white.

650 _ 0   *[blank]*
630 0 0   ≠a Language arts (Early childhood).

6.2.8. (10 errors)

         [blank] [kit]

245 0 0   ≠a Kindergarten basics in math. ≠h KIT .

260   ≠a Englewood Cliffs, N.J. : ≠b Scholastic, ≠c 1982.

         cards *[replace semicolons with commas (1 error)]*

300   ≠a 32 activity crds ; 1 mini-guide ; 12 parent component spirit masters (1 each in English and Spanish) ; 1 worksheet book ; 1 teaching guide, in box, 25 × 32 × 6 cm.

                    0
440   ①   ≠a Scholastic early childhood program

500   ≠a Title on teaching guide: Mathematics.

520
(530)   ≠a Presents mathematical concepts and introduces mathematics skills in an
             ordered sequence, from recognizing patterns to thinking logically.

                              ≠x
650   0   ≠a Arithmetic (≠b) Study and teaching (Primary)

246 3 _
(740 0 1)   ≠a Mathematics.

[delete this line and change the 440 second indicator to zero]
(830 0   ≠a Scholastic early childhood program.)

6.3. Kits, 008 (Header) Information Exercise Answers

6.3.1.   Form of item
          a.   c
          b.   f
          c.   r
          d.   a
          e.   d
          f.   b
          g.
6.3.2.   Modified record
          a.   d
          b.   s
          c.
          d.   x
          e.   o
          f.   o
6.3.3.   Date types
          a.   e
          b.   q
          c.   u
          d.   k
          e.
          f.   p

6.4. Kits, *AACR2R* Chapter 3 Exercise Answers

6.4.1.   As an item containing two or more categories of material, no one of which is predominant.

6.4.2.   Chapter 1, rule 1.10 (Items made up of several types of material).

6.4.3.   Give a general term as to the extent, such as "35 various pieces".

6.4.4.   Kits ; or, Multimedia.

6.4.5.   Give them together in one note, separated by period, space, dash, space.

6.4.6.   a) Give the extent of each part or group of parts in a general list, with the dimensions of the container if desired.

b) Give a separate physical description for each part or group of parts belonging to a distinct class of material, if desired. Give each one on a separate line.

7.1. Miscellaneous Nonprint, Full Records Tagging Exercise Answers

7.1.1.   245 0 4 ≠a The treasures of Tutankhamen ≠h [slide].

260   ≠a New York : ≠b Metropolitan Museum of Art, ≠c c1976.

300   ≠a 41 slides : ≠b col. ; ≠c 35 mm. + ≠e 1 sound cassette.

500   ≠a Sound accompaniment compatible with manual and automatic equipment.

520   ≠a Objects from the tomb of Tutankhamen including statuettes, masks richly inlaid with jewels, and funerary jewelry and furniture. Narrative explains each, tells its use, and gives a little Egyptian history from the time of Tutankhamen.

600 0 0 ≠a Tutankhamen, ≠c King of Egypt ≠x Tomb.

650   0 ≠a Art objects, Egyptian ≠x Exhibitions.

651   0 ≠a Egypt ≠x Antiquities ≠x Exhibitions.

710 2   ≠a Metropolitan Museum of Art (New York, N.Y.)

7.1.2.   245 0 0 ≠a Remembering college ≠h [kit].

260   ≠a New York : ≠b Bi-Folkal Productions, ≠c 1992.

300   ≠a 1 banner, 3 paperback books, 75 slides (in carousel), 3 art prints, 1 songbook (30 copies), 5 duplicating masters, 2 sound cassettes, and 1 videocassette, in bag 54 × 12 × 26 cm.

520   ≠a Designed to be used in nursing homes and retirement homes to stimulate memories and discussions among older persons.

650   0 ≠a Universities and colleges ≠x Miscellanea.

7.1.3.   100 1   ≠a Ormond, Mary Jane, ≠d 1941-

245 1 0 ≠a Houmas House ≠h [art reproduction] / ≠c Mary Jane Ormond.

260   ≠a New York : ≠b New York Reprographics, ≠c 1964.

300   ≠a 1 art print : ≠b col. ; ≠c 43 × 72 cm. on sheet 53 × 82 cm.

500   ≠a Reproduction of oil painting originally painted in 1962.

650   0 ≠a Houmas House Plantation (La.)

7.1.4.   245 0 0   ≠a Alaska ≠h [motion picture].

250   ≠a 2nd ed.

260   ≠a Portland, Ore. : ≠b Encounter Productions, ≠c c1984.

300   ≠a 1 film reel (30 min.) : ≠b sd., col. ; ≠c 16 mm.

440   0   ≠a International travel guides

520   ≠a Introduces viewers to Alaska's fascinating history and to such scenic wonders as Mount McKinley and Glacier Bay.

651   0   ≠a Alaska ≠x Description and travel.

7.1.5.   100 1   ≠a Lacey, Susan, ≠d 1944-

245 1 0   ≠a Body of evidence ≠h [microform] / ≠c by Susan Lee Lacey.

250   ≠a 1st ed.

260   ≠a New York : ≠b Apron Books, ≠c c1967.

300   ≠a 166 p. ; ≠c 22 cm.

500   ≠a Includes bibliographical references (p. 164-166).

533   ≠a Microfiche. ≠b Belleville, N.C. : ≠c Micrographico, ≠d 1985. ≠e 44 microfiches : positive ; 11 × 15 cm.

650   0   ≠a Murder ≠z New York (State) ≠z New York ≠x Case studies.